Teenage Boys and
High School English

Teenage Boys and High School English

Bruce Pirie

Foreword by Deborah Appleman

Boynton/Cook
HEINEMANN
Portsmouth, NH

Boynton/Cook Publishers, Inc.
A subsidiary of Reed Elsevier Inc.
361 Hanover Street
Portsmouth, NH 03801–3912
www.boyntoncook.com

Offices and agents throughout the world

The author and publisher wish to thank those who have generously given permission to reprint borrowed material:

A portion of Chapter 6 is adapted from *Reshaping School English* by Bruce Pirie. Copyright © 1997 by the National Council of Teachers of English. Reprinted by permission.

Excerpts adapted from "Untold Stories: Culture as Activity" by Bruce Pirie in *The English Record* 50.3 (Spring/Summer 2000). Copyright © 2000 by Bruce Pirie.

All teachers and students are identified by pseudonyms.

Cataloging-in-Publication (CIP) data is on file with the Library of Congress
ISBN 0-86709-536-9

Editor: Lisa Luedeke
Production editor: Sonja S. Chapman
Cover design: Night & Day Design
Typesetter: House of Equations, Inc.
Manufacturing: Steve Bernier

Printed in the United States of America on acid-free paper
06 05 04 03 02 RRD 1 2 3 4 5

For Julian,
my own boy

Human beings must invent themselves in the midst of an infinity of possibilities, instead of passively accepting their roles because they think they could not be other than they are.

—Augusto Boal

Contents

Foreword by Deborah Appleman ix

Acknowledgments xiii

Chapter 1   Why Bother? 1

Chapter 2   Why Are They Like That? 9

Chapter 3   Classroom Visit: *Grade 11, Nonacademic* 22

Chapter 4   Wuss! *Dealing with Feelings* 33

Chapter 5   Voodoo and Gibber-Jabber: *Writing* 51

Chapter 6   I Have Better Things to Do: *Reading* 76

Chapter 7   Classroom Visit: *Grade 10, Academic* 101

Chapter 8   They Just Don't Listen! *Speaking and Listening* 111

Chapter 9   Classroom Visit: *Grade 9, Academic* 126

Chapter 10   An Infinity of Possibilities 133

Works Cited 145

Foreword

Teenage Boys and high school English. Before this phrase became the title of Bruce Pirie's important new book, it was a combination of words that often worried the hearts of English teachers everywhere.

Three weeks into my own career of teaching high school English, I found myself calling my younger brother in desperation. It was the first time in our lives that I had ever asked him for advice. (Shame on me.) "What did you like to read when you were in high school?" I implored. "My male students hate everything I pick out." "Try anything by Tolkien or Louis L'Amour" he offered. "They worked for me. And try being well, more cool and less lady-teacherish. That would help, too." Of course, his advice didn't hold true for every boy. But to me, my brother had insider knowledge, a secret key to a club to which I could never belong. My lack of membership in that club and my ignorance of gender issues in teaching English made me, for the first few years of my high school teaching career, a better teacher of teenage girls than of teenage boys.

From text selection to classroom management, the presence of teenage boys in high school English classes gives my preservice English education students the most pause. "Can I teach *The House on Mango Street?*" they ask. "There are 18 boys and 6 girls in that class." "The girls seem to be accepting me as a teacher but the boys are not buying it. What should I do?" "How can I make journal writing seem relevant to boys?" "What do boys like to read, anyway?" "How can I create classroom discussions where male and female voices can be equally heard?" "Why do so many of my boy students seem bored with whatever I do in English class?" "Do boys hate poetry, or am I choosing the wrong poems?"

In my recent visits to high school English classroom across our country, I've noticed disturbing trends that confirm our growing concern about the match between our current literacy instructional practices and the interests and achievement of adolescent males. Advanced Placement or "college bound" English classes are too frequently primarily female, while "remedial" reading classes are disproportionately filled with boys. What is it about our practices and our curricula that have failed to engage half of the student population? And, what can we do to stem the negative discourse that has become commonplace when people speak of teenage boys and high school English?

We are riding a new cultural wave of concern about boys and literacy. Tomes about boys abound, from the reactionary (Hoff Sommers' *The War against the Boys*, 2000) to the plaintive, (Biddulph's *Raising Boys*, 1997). Most recently, Smith and Wilhelm (2002) offer a provocative exploration of literacy in the lives of young men and suggest how we might alter our instructional practices to make them more responsive to the needs, expectations, and predispositions of young men. As Smith and Wilhelm argue: "If boys are not embracing literacy, we want to think hard about what we can do to help them" (p. xx). Smith and Wilhelm also caution us not to echo the polarized language of the "gender wars " but to think deeply and carefully about individual male students and their literacy lives. In this book, Bruce Pirie gives us the tools to do just that.

In *Teenage Boys and High School English*, Pirie begins by offering a compelling argument for why it is important to concern ourselves with the literacy achievements of adolescent males. Despite the common and often stridently stated sentiment that boys belong to a younger subset of the still-privileged class of males, Pirie argues powerfully that we need to examine our literacy practices so that boys will feel that our English classrooms are safe, fair, and productive places in which both teenage boys and teenage girls can thrive and grow.

Pirie 's points are effectively animated by lively "classroom visits" that ring achingly true. Readers will recognize the poignant portraits of teachers and students negotiating the turbulent waters of adolescent identity and literary knowing with texts like *Catcher in the Rye, Lord of the Flies*, and *Hamlet* as their shaky yet durable bridges. Pirie brings to life the unarticulated yet real worries of teachers who often notice the teenage boys in their high school English classrooms but don't want to admit the patterns that they see, even to themselves.

Perhaps the most important contributions of this book are the practical strategies Pirie offers to teachers. These wise suggestions are grounded in well-researched theory and tested by Pirie's own practice. For example, Pirie offers the use of drama in the English classroom as a way of deflecting and redirecting the energy of students in the classroom. Similarly, he provides a way of thinking through writing essays from "the ground up" that might be a more compatible heuristic for the way many boys like to think. To avoid common adolescent male aversion to the notion that writing poetry is a feminine expression of feelings, Pirie advocates using published poems that are tied thematically to another text that is under study. As you read this book you will discover many, many straightforward strategies whose genius lie in their simplicity and in their acknowledgment of some of the learning preferences and stances of teen-age boys.

In the opening paragraphs of this forward, I confessed that in my early days as a high school teacher I was a better teacher of girls than I was of boys. If I had been able to read this book, that might not have been true for long. Pirie delivers on the promise he makes in Chapter 1 to provide readers with a "richer understanding of what it means to be a teen-age boy today and a deeper appreciation of the qualities boys can bring to the English classroom." He gives teachers a glimpse into his own successful practices and provides us with the tools to create our own set of strategies as well. His final chapter, aptly titled "An Infinity of Possibilities," offers us a way to reconsider the gendered elements in our practices, in texts, and in the degree to which we may be complicit in the construction of our students' interpretations of gender and identity. Thanks to Pirie's courageous and insightful contribution, things are beginning to look up for teenage boys in their high school English classrooms. And when things look up for high school boys, we all benefit.

—Deborah Appleman
Carleton College

Acknowledgments

I must thank my wife, Jennifer Mansell, who is, as always, my first reader and critic.

I especially appreciate the kindness of the colleagues who allowed me to visit their classes for the "classroom visit" chapters, and the students and parents who granted permission for student writing to be reproduced.

1 *Why Bother?*

"You're writing a book about helping boys?" a colleague asked doubtfully. "Why would you bother? Don't men have advantages enough already?"

Her skepticism is understandable. In May of 2000, the cover of *The Atlantic Monthly* provocatively declared, "Girls RULE!" but in truth they don't, not in ways that we all know matter. Women's average salaries still don't match men's, and men dominate powerful boardrooms and legislatures. To speak of an overall male disadvantage in the modern world would be disingenuous. At least for the moment, boys are far more likely than girls to grow up and become president of the United States, CEO of a major corporation, or winner of a Nobel Prize.

However, males also figure disproportionately in other statistics. Congress may be packed with men, but so is the prison system. Boys are more likely than girls to die by accident before the end of their teenage years. They are more likely to "successfully" commit suicide or be diagnosed with mental, emotional, learning, or behavioral problems. Boys dominate schools' lists of "problem" students: they are much more likely to fail, be suspended, be expelled, or drop out of school (Gurian 1998, 11–15).

When I talk with teachers about boys' typically weaker academic achievement, especially in the subject English, they often say something like, "Still, you know, in my grade 12 class, there are two excellent boys. They're probably the top students in the room." There are, of course, boys who do well in English. When conventional measures of intelligence are applied, boys' scores typically cluster less around the mean; instead of the traditional bell curve, the graph of boys' intelligence is a flattened curve, with fewer individuals at the center and more at the extremes (Head 1999, 63). This helps explain why there are always a number of excellent male students in our schools. Top boys make a strong impression on us, but whenever I look at statistics in my school or from around the world, it turns out that those memorable boys are exceptions. A good way to begin work in this area is to compile achievement statistics for your own school or district. Individual classrooms may vary, but as your sample gets larger, you are likely to find a pretty clear picture emerging: the top ranks will be dominated by girls and the bottom ranks appallingly packed by boys.

In real terms, exactly how big is this gender gap in literacy? Statistics can be slippery, and when we're playing with numbers, a couple of things must be remembered. First, we are talking about *average* scores; obviously many individual boys score better than some individual girls, even if overall trends favor girls. Second, gender isn't the only issue. Other factors such as parents' education and ethnicity, which are often markers of economic status, figure in here as well, sometimes to a much greater extent than sex. In other words, individual achievement emerges from within a complex nest of variables, only one of which is the student's sex. With those reservations in mind, we can try to make sense of the numbers.

Reading Scores

The federally commissioned National Assessment of Educational Progress (NAEP, or The Nation's Report Card) has produced statistics for three decades. NAEP grades reading on a scale of 500. A student reaching Level 200 is described as being "able to understand, combine ideas, and make inferences based on short uncomplicated passages about specific or sequentially related information." This seems a modest goal, and in 1999, 96 percent of grade 8 girls achieved at least that level, compared to 91 percent of boys—a spread of 5 percentage points. When we raise the bar to Level 250 ("able to search for specific information, interrelate ideas, and make generalizations about literature, science, and social studies materials") the gap widens to 11 percent: 66 percent of girls but only 55 percent of boys reached this level.

That's as the students are about to enter high school. We expect them all to grow in the years of secondary education, but does that gap close? Apparently not. By grade 12, 87 percent of girls but only 77 percent of boys made it to Level 250—still 10 percentage points apart. The next rung on the ladder, Level 300 ("able to find, understand, summarize, and explain relatively complicated literary and informational material"), was attained by 45 percent of grade 12 girls but, predictably, by only 34 percent of boys. While gaps between racial and ethnic groups shrank in the '70s and '80s, *the pattern of gender differences described here—the spread of about 10 percentage points when we ask who is reaching the higher levels of reading achievement—has been rock solid since the first comparable reports in 1971* (NCES 2001, 132).

Writing Scores

In 1998, NAEP tested students on three kinds of writing tasks: narrative, informative, and persuasive. The results were rated as "basic," "proficient," or "advanced," then translated to a 300-point scale, with 150 as the national average. Grade 8 boys scored, on average, 140, or 10 points below the national average. Grade 8 girls scored 160—10 points above the average. The results for grade 12 were almost identical: boys 140, girls 159.

Using the same data, NAEP asked what percentages of students were at or above the "proficient" level: in grade 8, 17 percent of boys and 36 percent of girls were at least proficient; in grade 12, 14 percent of boys and 29 percent of girls were at least proficient (NCES 1999, 10). To put those figures as starkly as possible, *there are about twice as many girls as boys at the "proficient" or "advanced" levels of writing in the high school years.*

This is not an exclusively American phenomenon. U.S. statistics mirror results from around the English-speaking world. In Canada, the province of Ontario has just initiated a grade 10 literacy test that will be a requirement for graduation. In its first administration, nearly 70 percent of girls but only 55 percent of boys passed both the reading and writing components of the test (EQAO 2001b). Britain has been paying attention to this issue for a decade, and its Office for Standards in Education notes that girls get off to a better start in the primary grades and hold on to that lead throughout school. By the time they are enrolled in secondary English, two-thirds of girls in England are scoring in the top achievement levels (A to C standings), compared to fewer than half of the boys (Arnot et al. 1998, 9). A study of both participation and achievement in Australia flatly concluded that girls "perform better than boys in English across all criteria in all states and across all types of examination questions" (Teese et al. 1995, 94). Indeed, a major study of 250,000 fifteen-year-olds in thirty-two countries (and seventeen different languages) found girls universally achieving higher reading scores (Bussière et al. 2001, 25).

Attitudes

Such discrepancies in our students' achievement ought to challenge teachers of English and language arts, but what I find even more worrying are indicators of boys' *attitudes* toward the subject. We know that many boys don't feel as comfortable in English as girls do—certainly not as comfortable as they feel in math or science. One research project investigated attitudes toward math and English among 650 American students from grade 7 to 12. Three factors were measured: students' self-concept of ability in the subject, their rating of the worth of the subject, and their interest in the subject. As one might predict, girls scored significantly higher on all attitudinal measures related to English. In math, boys had more positive attitudes than girls, but the differences weren't nearly as large as the attitude differences toward English (Watt and Eccles 1999).

Once again, these findings are consistent with results from other English-speaking countries. The study cited earlier found comparable attitudes among Australian teenagers, and British researchers are well aware that boys are less enthusiastic both about the school subject and about reading and writing in general (OFSTED 1993; Millard 1997).

One tangible measure of attitude is course selection. In English-speaking countries, the subject English is compulsory for most of the school years, but what happens when students have a choice? In 1994, when American high school transcripts were tabulated, noticeably more girls than boys were choosing to take Advanced Placement English: a difference of 5.43 percent, by far the largest enrollment difference by sex in AP courses reported for that year (NCES 1998, A-193). As students move on to university, these preferences are confirmed: women graduating with bachelor's or master's degrees in English outnumber men by about two to one (NCES 2001, 313). Many of those graduates, of course, have no interest in returning to teach school English. These days, teaching of any subject attracts fewer male candidates, and the National Council of Teachers of English reports that, at the secondary level, only 17 percent of its members are male (Kelley 2001). There have been years when I have been one of only two men in a department of ten or twelve teachers in total.

These statistics suggest that English is perceived as a girls' subject. Many students will tell us that in their own words, none more bluntly than a low-achieving grade 10 student in Australia. Teacher Wayne Martino asked his students to write what they thought of the subject, and Brad wrote:

> *I don't like English . . . it's not the way guys think . . . This subject is the biggest load of utter bullshit I have ever done. Therefore, I don't particularly like this subject. I hope you aren't offended by this, but most guys who like English are faggots. (Martino 1995, 129)*

In its own way, Brad's comment is worth a shelf full of government studies. I don't suppose most boys feel as strongly as Brad, but his contempt strikes a note that echoes throughout both the international research and my own work. Some boys feel they are being asked to think in ways that they don't find easy or even desirable. They may doubt the validity of the work they are asked to do or feel anxious about its apparent open-endedness. English may seem less safe than science or math because, in the words of some grade 11 boys, "there is no definite answer," and it all "depends on your view of things," whereas science is "straightforward" because "there are no shades to it." Science and math offer solid learning about worthwhile, tangible topics, but English perversely insists on venturing into the murky area of feelings: "When you read a book, it's like delving into people's lives. It's being nosey" (Pugh 1995, 19). And underneath it all lies the suspicion that this subject, so often taught by women, is somehow unmanly, or as Brad says, "not the way guys think." In a culture that defines masculinity as being *not* feminine, it is inevitable that some boys will treat this subject as they treat other things identified as feminine—that is, with responses that range from fear and suspicion to hostility and contempt.

We can compare this to the problem of "girls in math" that began attracting attention a few decades ago. It never really was a case of girls not being able to do math. They always were capable; the problem lay in their attitudes toward themselves and the subject. Girls didn't see themselves as mathematicians. They dropped the subject as soon as they could and certainly didn't target futures that would require the use of complicated mathematics. As a result, girls cut themselves off from a range of careers that might have brought them both happiness and material success. Educators influenced by the women's movement naturally saw these attitudes as an obstacle to be overcome, and they set to work, experimenting with more "girl-friendly" approaches and recruiting more women teachers into what had previously been a male discipline.

Their effort made a difference. The American Association of University Women has documented and welcomed clear signs of improvement in girls' scores and enrollment in math. At the same time they have flagged technology as a new challenge in girls' education: "A discouraging new gap is emerging, as computer science becomes the new 'boys' club'" (AAUW 1998, 4).

At the heart of this book is my conviction that it is now time for educators to address the difficulties of boys in English with the same energy and commitment that have been applied so successfully to the problem of girls in math.

Some will say that boys are *innately* inferior in language work, so what can a teacher hope to do? Some also said that about girls in math. In truth, there may be innate differences, and in the next chapter, we'll look at that question. For now, however, note that math teachers refused to use that as an excuse to give up on girls. They knew that whatever might be the inherent strengths in male or female brains, there were obviously so many attitudes standing in the way that girls clearly weren't achieving all that they could. Those teachers knew that more was possible and understood that teaching was about building possibilities rather than surrendering to the limitations of biology or the past.

Some will say that these attitudes are built from infancy in the home, in the elementary schools, and in the culture at large. Isn't adolescence too late to be trying to make a difference? It *is* late, and all those other areas do need attention. But I teach high school. I do that because this is where I figure that I, with my personality and my interests, have a chance to make a difference in the world. If you're a secondary teacher, I hope you too believe that about yourself. I've seen enough students take sudden new interest in reading and writing (or math, science, music, history, drama, or whatever) to reaffirm my faith that adolescents can still grow and change, that high schools are places that can make such growth happen, and that teachers can make a difference.

The Motivation for Change

Girls had good, obvious reasons to take up math: it was easy to point to long lists of well-paid occupations that require a math background. When you're on the second rung in society, it's not all that hard to see why you might want to change the way you're doing things. It's different for boys. As I said at the beginning, men as a group are not disadvantaged in some of the most material ways. There may be a subclass of illiterates on the street and in prison, but for most men, not doing as well in English as their female classmates doesn't seem to have hurt them at all. In fact, if anything, it has only proven that they're "real guys."

Where, then, is the motivation for boys to change? If the problem is that boys don't buy into this subject, we have to be prepared to *sell* it. If we have to argue on economic grounds, I think we can. Lower-level literacy may have served well enough for the old industrial economy, but as the new economy pushes unskilled and semiskilled jobs out to workers in the developing world, future employment in major western nations will increasingly demand more sophisticated thinking and communication skills. What counts as adequate literacy has been historically defined by the changing needs of society and its economy. Miles Myers (1996) has traced this history and argues that we now face the challenge of developing a new critical literacy. Yesterday's version of English studies may not matter much for success in the new market, but as the subject transforms itself into a training ground for crucial ways of thinking and communicating, both boys and girls will need full mastery of the tools we can offer.

That's the marketplace argument, but English teachers probably also believe that our subject is about more than positioning students for the job market. English is important for our students as *people*. Boys who don't buy in to the values of the subject are, we fear, losing something that matters more than career opportunities. They're cutting themselves off from ways of thinking and feeling that are important in their humanity. The young men and women in our classrooms will be making the future, and we want them to be good spouses, parents, leaders, and visionaries. As I write this, I have an eight-year-old son. I want him to grow up to be a man whose life is enriched by the values of the subject I teach.

Backlash Politics

In these opening pages, I've tried to answer voices that might ask, "Why bother working on the problem of boys in English?" There is one more skeptical voice that I have to answer. When one of my fellow teachers told a friend about the work I was doing, her friend exploded, "I can't stand it! All that 'boy' stuff is just a lot of right-wing, antifeminist backlash!" My colleague was taken aback by the vehemence of the attack, especially since, knowing me, she was sure that "right-wing" and "antifeminist" hardly describe my leanings. But there is such a thing as antifeminist backlash out there, and teachers interested in boys' education have to separate themselves carefully from such motivations.

Part of the problem arises when we start talking about *advantage* versus *disadvantage*, making education seem like a tug-of-war for a limited supply of benefits. Men had advantages in many areas of life, and then the women's movement came along and seemed to be trying to take those advantages away from men. In a new round of gender wars, some warriors now try to reclaim for boys what they supposedly lost. This combative frame of mind can be seen in the debate sparked by *The War Against Boys: How Misguided Feminism Is Harming Our Young Men*, in which Christina Hoff Sommers (2000) launches an inflammatory attack against some of the earlier advocates for girls and provokes a counterattack from those advocates, played out on the letters pages of *The Atlantic Monthly* during August of 2000. Classroom teachers aren't likely to gain much practical help from this political squabble. Our job is to help *all* students do their best, and learning doesn't have to be seen as a commodity in limited supply, stingily doled out to either side of a balancing scale—a spoonful more for the boys, taken away from the little pile for girls. In fact, by the time you've read Chapter 2, I hope you'll agree that a better education for boys will also be exactly what is best suited for large numbers of girls. When we stop thinking in terms of a polarized war, we can have winners all around the table.

In later chapters, I pull together research and thinking about boys in English from around the world. Much of the material comes, as you will see, from Britain and Australia, where teachers identified the problem earlier than we have in North America. Ultimately, this is not a book of theory, but a book about practice. When I read the research, I measure it for practicality against the work I do in my own (mixed-sex) secondary English classroom. Sometimes I've been successful in engaging boys; sometimes I haven't. I'll show you things I've tried, and I'll offer you approaches that take advantage of research and theory and remain true to my own classroom experience.

By the time you finish this book, you should have an understanding of major issues in boys' education. You may have a richer understanding of what it means to be a teenage boy today and a deeper appreciation of the qualities boys can bring to the English classroom. You will certainly have an initial set of strategies to which you will, no doubt, add your own.

2 *Why Are They Like That?*

How does a boy become a *boy*? We don't have to retrace all the steps in the nature versus nurture debate, but how we understand the roots of gendered behavior affects how we teach. If we think that boys have a genetic antipathy for the work of the English classroom, we might shrug our shoulders, sigh, and say, "Boys will be boys. What else did you expect?" Or we might decide that since there's no use fighting nature, we should reform the subject instead, masculinizing English until it is palatable for boys. But then what happens to the girls? Are we prepared to offer two versions of English—Boys English and Girls English—in classrooms segregated by sex?

On the other hand, if we believe that gender traits are learned through some process of socialization, we may be more ready to try to undo the process, but aren't we setting ourselves up for quixotic failure if we tilt against the windmills of a lifetime of enculturation? And how would we answer the charge that we're dabbling with social engineering, presuming to revise the very nature of masculinity, instead of sticking to our jobs as schoolteachers?

In this chapter, I sketch in the larger context for boys' difficulties with literacy. It is a picture that is still being debated and clarified, but we know enough to begin mapping a path.

Biology and the Brain

It's natural to look for quick answers to complex questions, and biology is one popular explanation for learning differences. It is obvious that men and women are built differently, so isn't it reasonable to expect those differences to extend to the brain as well? This type of explanation has particular appeal in the mass media, where simple ideas win audiences. After all, if you were a magazine editor, which screaming headline would you rather run on your cover—"Scientists Unlock the Literacy Gene" or

"Literacy Potential Turns Out to Be a Complex and Subtle Interaction of Various Factors, Highly Dependent on Context and Amenable to No Single Fix"?

Popular biological, or "brain-based," explanations sometimes oversimplify the issues. To take one particularly contentious example, testosterone is a favorite hormone for those seeking the key to boys' actions. It is credited or blamed for competitive and aggressive behavior. After a rough day in a classroom full of teenage boys, exhausted teachers will say, "Too much testosterone in that room!" We imagine that uncontrollable squirts of testosterone take over our boys, as if alien body snatchers were at work, turning otherwise decent young men into brawling, boastful studs.

The truth turns out to be more complicated. In *The Two Sexes*, distinguished psychologist Eleanor Maccoby reminds us that most aggressive behavior patterns are developed in the years *before* puberty, as early as age three, when there isn't any difference in the low levels of male hormones found in both little girls and little boys (1998, 35). When eight- or nine-year-old boys scrap on the playground, it isn't because they've just had a testosterone rush. In fact, as they head into puberty, when those hormones do appear, many of those same boys will tame down their rough play (37).

Does that dissolve any link between testosterone and aggression? Not quite. Although young children don't have floods of sex-specific hormones, there are prenatal bursts of hormone production. Possibly, the infant's brain is already primed *in utero* to be receptive to certain kinds of experiences. This hypothesis is supported by experiments in which pregnant monkeys injected with testosterone produced offspring—even female offspring—more likely to engage in rough play. In humans, there have been studies of females with adreno genital syndrome (AGS), a condition caused by the release of excess androgens (male hormones) during the fetal period. Their genital abnormality can be corrected surgically, but these girls retain a preference for masculine play behavior—more rough play and less interest in dolls (Maccoby 1998, 112).

However, a still further complication can be seen in research that tracked a large group of boys from ages six to thirteen. Teachers, peers, and researchers rated the boys on their levels of aggression and their "social dominance"—the extent to which they were perceived as popular leaders. At age thirteen, these boys were tested several times during the day for testosterone levels. Interestingly, boys who were the *most* aggressive, but who were having the least success in school and socially, were found to have *low* levels of testosterone. Socially dominant but nonaggressive boys had *higher* levels of testosterone. In the words of the researchers, "High testosterone levels in adolescent boys may thus be regarded as a marker of social success in a given context, rather than of social maladjustment as suggested in previous studies" (Schaal et al. 1996, 1322).

This is consistent with a growing belief among psychologists that testosterone production is stimulated by external events (Head 1999, 13; Kindlon and Thompson 1999, 14). More testosterone shows up in men *as* they experience success, whether it be in the boxing ring, at the chessboard, in a political debate, or on the stock market. The hormonal change seems connected with a pleasurable feeling of well-being that is the *result* of success, rather than the *cause* of competitive behavior.

Thus, the research results cited earlier make sense: boys who are the most socially successful have that sense of well-being and the higher levels of testosterone that go with it. In fact, the more aggressive boys may be driven to fighting and bullying precisely because they have low testosterone levels: they have to make themselves feel good somehow, and if social and academic achievement is denied to them, beating someone up in a fight may be their one way of getting a little blip of success. That's a strategy for making themselves feel better. Strategies are learned, and they've learned a strategy different than the one learned by more socially successful boys. They learned it not from hormones in the bloodstream, but from the violence that is glamorized in the mass media and in some peer cultures.

In short, it's too simple to say, "Boys have testosterone and that's why they're more aggressive and competitive." The connection isn't automatic: there is a context of learning and culture that intervenes.

Another issue that invites biological explanation is the question of girls' earlier language development. There does seem to be evidence of a female head start: girls begin to talk earlier than boys, and, as toddlers, may talk more than boys, at least to other girls. Eleanor Maccoby puts this cautiously, reporting that "there are hints of a neural substrate that enables girls to progress faster (or at least differently) with respect to language" (1998, 107). The early neural advantage, however, fades, and the small differences in mature brains don't explain the persistent differences in achievement and attitude.

There is growing agreement that women's brain activity typically involves more of the brain, while men's brains operate more in specialized, localized areas. This may be why some women recover more quickly from strokes: perhaps their brains, with a habit of generalized activity, more easily compensate when one area is damaged (Gurian 1998, 17). However, it's not entirely clear what this difference would mean for educators. The male specialized pattern is sometimes credited for helping with spatial tasks, while the female global tendency supposedly helps with language work, but why exactly should those brain patterns align with those thinking tasks? Is there some advantage to one style over the other? These questions are unanswered (Head 1999, 15).

Brain differences become especially interesting when we ask how language is used to process feelings. The difficulty that many men have expressing their feelings in words is widely recognized, and this creates an obvious problem for the subject of English. If you're going to use language for self-expression and if you're going to talk about literature, you can't very well avoid talking about feelings, and this is exactly the aspect of the subject that bothers some boys (Martino 1995, 127). There has been plenty written about emotion and language centers in the brain, although it should be pointed out that while specific motor functions may be mapped onto particular areas of the brain, the more complex functions of language, feeling, and learning seem less easily pinned down (Head 1999, 14). In the past, it has been reported that the corpus callosum—the bundle of fibers connecting the right and left hemispheres of the brain—is larger in women than in men; this supposedly meant that emotional data more easily connects with the language processing center in women's brains. (See, for example, Moir and Jessel 1991, 48.) However, the past few years have seen great advances in brain research, and it's no longer so clear that the corpus callosum is, in fact, typically larger in women than in men (Gilbert and Gilbert 1998, 38–39).

Sometimes evolutionary explanations are offered. For example, if women at one time had to stay home to care for children while men went out to hunt and kill, it would make sense for women's brains to develop greater sensitivity to the feelings of others. This enhanced sensitivity does seem to exist, as studies repeatedly find women better able to identify emotional states in others (Goleman 1995, 97). Evolution could help explain some men's aversion to talking about feelings. At a time when men were hunters and warriors, they needed to take immediate action, not spend time talking about their feelings. If you're on a battlefield, it's not helpful to pull out your response journal; you'd better just pull out your battle-ax and slug the other guy. You can talk about it later.

What the World Demands of Us

Whatever the biological and evolutionary givens, for us as teachers it may be more important to understand that much recent research points to the brain's ability to *grow and change in response to the environment. That is, the things that our brains practice, they become better at.* John Head (1999) addresses this crucial concept when he points out that even if brain function is a cause of sex differences in language ability, there are two possibilities that ensue.

One hypothesis is that boys and girls are born with different brains. The other possibility is that different skills develop through different experiences and use of the brain. This latter possibility is consistent with our knowledge about how the brain functions. Most brain growth occurs early in life. If the brain is not fully used then some of its functions literally atrophy; the neurons do not connect up with each other. If, in other cases, an experience is repeated, so that it becomes a routine, strong neural pathways are established, so that the operation becomes easier. (14–15)

That means that the question becomes What kinds of experiences do we subject young children to? Do boys and girls have early experiences different enough to develop different capacities in their brains?

We know that, despite our best intentions to be gender neutral, there is a common tendency for parents to have more elaborated, in-depth talk about feelings with female children (Maccoby 1998, 146–47). Emotion talk with boys typically deals with a narrower range of feelings, often focusing on anger. Indeed, parents are likely to have more talk of any kind with female babies (Head 1999, 22). This early interaction presumably makes a difference in developing the capacity and inclination to use the language of feelings and even to pay attention to feelings. If girls get more early practice at articulating their feelings, we shouldn't be surprised if teenage boys are at a loss for words when asked to identify emotional states—their own or others'. That doesn't mean that men can't *learn* to recognize and articulate feelings. Daniel Goleman, author of *Emotional Intelligence*, insists that these skills can be nurtured, in men as well as women: "Indeed, a major review of data on male-female sex differences argues that men have as much latent ability for empathy, but less motivation to be empathic, than do in women" (1998, 323). The lack of motivation comes from living in a macho culture that identifies emotion talk as feminine.

We also know that children in elementary and middle school identify the practice of reading with women. It is the mothers who read books and magazines for pleasure and who are more likely to cuddle up in bed and read a story with their children. When fathers read, it is typically only newspapers or material brought home from work (Millard 1997, 11–12; Pottorff, Phelps-Zientarski, and Skovera 1996, 209). Children get pretty clear messages about who does and does not get involved in reading, and this of course affects their willingness to practice reading.

As you can see, in this chapter I have been moving away from biological explanations and toward recognition of the cultural factors that shape boys' and girls' attitudes. I don't mean to deny the existence of biology. That would be foolish. Yes, teenage boys have testosterone spikes (even though we don't fully understand the significance of that fact). Yes, there are some different patterns in the workings of male and female brains, and yes, girls may have a predisposition to earlier language development.

I can't do much about any of those things. However, whatever might be the students' native ability, the next question is what happens with that ability, and that depends on a lot of people's *attitudes* to things like reading, writing, talking, and reflecting about language and about inner experience. There is the attitude of the student and his or her peers, the attitudes of the parents, the attitude of the culture, and my attitude as a teacher. Those attitudes spell out the possibilities that we are willing to imagine for each student, the expectations and dreams that we allow and encourage. As a teacher, I focus my effort at that crucial point of possibility where ability meets attitude.

Let me put that more concretely. The authors of one of these studies point out that kids with little innate ability in a field often persevere and do well despite a slow start: boys with little athletic ability sometimes doggedly persist in sports until they become reasonable—maybe not outstanding, but reasonable—athletes (Pottorff, Phelps-Zientarski, and Skovera 1996, 209). Their motivation is inspired and supported by a culture that endorses sports as a masculine activity. That support is precisely what is missing from reading when boys see mainly their mothers doing pleasurable reading, when their fathers and brothers are more likely to tell them to put aside the books and join a ball game outside, when the images of reading in popular culture are more likely to show girls with books (cited in Millard 1997, 19), and when most literacy teachers in elementary and secondary school are women. For many boys, girls seem to have a head start in reading and writing. That gap could be closed if the boys were motivated, and some boys are, because they get the right mix of support and expectation, but others, in effect, ask themselves why they would want to work at those skills. Wouldn't that make them seem more like girls? Does our culture hold that up as a desirable goal?

Michael Gurian, in *A Fine Young Man*, says, "When something is wired into the brain, making it an ally is better than fighting it" (1998, 45). I'm sure that's true, but what I'm arguing here is that we want to be careful about too quickly or totally ascribing boys' (or anyone's) behavior, strengths, or weaknesses to inner "wiring." We all *learn* to make sense of the world through the interplay of what's inside us with all the stuff that's outside us—the options and resources that our homes, schools, and cultures make available to us. We certainly do want to respect scientific knowledge about what goes on inside people, but we also need to remember that teachers and schools play a crucial contextual role.

Masculine Plural: An Ongoing Improvisation

A very helpful writer for anyone trying to understand the construction of masculinity is R. W. Connell, especially in his books *Masculinities* (1995) and *The Men and the Boys* (2000). Connell warns us to be careful about the power of metaphors to shape the way we understand the world. For example, in the biological argument, people are "wired" or "programmed" to act in certain ways (1995, 48); for those who believe that we are passively "conditioned" by society to play out gender roles, the body is "a canvas to be painted, a surface to be imprinted, a landscape to be marked out" (50). For Connell, neither set of metaphors recognizes the fluidity of gender identities. We assemble and revise a collection of *practices*—ways of being masculine or feminine—in configurations that shift as we move from context to context and as we move through our lives: "The important thing is the *process* of configuring practice" (72).

Biology matters and socialization matters, but the boys in our classes are also actively thinking and experimenting, working through how to be male, just as the girls are working through how to be female. They are trying out roles, and the ideas for these roles come from their families, their ethnic backgrounds, their churches, their neighborhoods, and popular culture, which offers an immense and confusing array of gendered images.

Because the possibilities are so varied, there are always multiple masculinities at play in a given situation, even within the same individual, and these forms of masculinity struggle for dominance (Connell 2000, 10; Mac an Ghaill 1994, 51–88). Schools are one of the arenas where these struggles play themselves out. Depending on your neighborhood and school, you may see a Hispanic style of masculinity, an African American style, a wealthy style, a ghetto style, a jock style, a young entrepreneur style, and so on. We may be aware of these as factions, each marking out its own territory in the cafeteria and its own place in the school hierarchy. We also see individuals playing with elements from various styles, trying to assemble an identity from what may have been contradictory elements, as when white students pick up the hip-hop clothes and manners of what was originally a black cultural form. Pity the outsider—the recent immigrant, or even a newcomer from a school on the other side of town, or a homosexual student—trying to figure out what to wear, how to talk, how to move, how to fit into the hierarchy of masculinities at your school.

When you walk through the front door of my school, you're greeted by a banner proclaiming this to be the "Home of the Spartans" and featuring the profile of a man's head in what is vaguely a Greco-Roman military helmet. This Spartan head is a caricature of a fierce fighting brute, with a massive jutting jaw. All the school teams, male and female, use the Spartan name, but, as in many schools, boys football carries the most prestige. The school has a history of winning football championships, and being on that team offers boys a route to proud, physical, competitive masculinity.

On the other hand, with a special program for gifted students, our school also has a reputation for top-flight academic achievement. As they approach their senior year, students develop an increasing respect for success in school. Last year, I saw students putting up posters congratulating friends on being accepted into Ivy League universities. Some students perceive a contradiction between the academic reputation and the belligerent Spartan logo and try to define themselves as being in one or the other camp; others try to keep a foot in both worlds. This can lead to tensions. "Are you going to be in the band this year, or are you trying out for football?" is more than a time management problem: it is a question of identity.

There are many varieties of masculinity (and femininity) at work in any setting, but we can also recognize that in our culture there is a collection of traits that converge to form a dominant version of masculinity, a version with enough clout that it can't be ignored, and even boys who opt for alternative styles can't completely discount this powerful set of expectations. This dominant masculinity includes traditional expectations that a man will be strong, tough, athletic, commanding, competitive, a lone Marlboro cowboy sometimes, an aggressive team player at other times. He likes to drive fast and take risks. He doesn't like the color pink, and his eyes are cold. He handles weapons and machines better than he handles infants. He likes to display his muscles, not his emotions (other than anger), and he certainly doesn't cry. He puts forward a confident face and wears physical wounds proudly. He's not a sissy and gets insulted if you call him a "girl" or a "woman." Soldiers, athletes, and superheroes are the archetypes of his dreams. He's not a geek or a nerd, and he is not gay. He would rather fight than talk because he likes action better than words.

And he knows that reading books is something girls do.

Thanks to the women's movement, we've all come a long way in the past three decades, and that list of macho traits sounds like a parody, doesn't it? Feminists taught girls that they could be more than a narrow list of stereotypes—the traits that complement the macho list (submissiveness, gentleness, emotionality, and so on). However, even if it sounds satirical to read out such a list today, that doesn't mean the ideal has disappeared. This dominant masculinity—"hegemonic masculinity," as

Connell (1995) calls it—is a standard against which other forms of masculinity have to be measured. Computer geeks, for example, have seen their stock rise lately, but to be on safe ground, their practice has to include traits from the dominant set, including "mechanical ability" and "competitiveness." The computer geek may read voraciously, but his reading will be computer magazines and manuals, not novels about relationships.

One alternative ideal has gained such prominence that we should perhaps call it the new subdominant masculinity. I'm speaking, of course, of the "new man" —the sensitive guy who will cuddle babies and reveal tender emotions, and is as likely to write poetry as ride a motorcycle. The boys in our classrooms are aware of this ideal and know that it's what many girls and women would like them to be. They're also aware that it's not what many of their male classmates respect. Boys often confess that they talk one way in front of girls and another way in the locker room.

I saw the struggle between these competing versions of masculinity played out in the local video store. Ahead of me in the checkout line was a young man, maybe nineteen or twenty years old. As we waited to be served, a friend of his entered the store and greeted him.

"Hey, Brian!"

"Hi! How ya doing?"

"Great, great! Good game last night?"

"Yeah, really. Good stuff."

"Right. So . . . getting a movie?"

"Uh, yeah."

Brian suddenly became uncomfortable and adjusted his hand in a way that seemed meant to conceal the cover of the videotape he was holding. His friend was not to be put off, however.

"So, like, what's the movie?"

Plainly embarrassed, Brian showed the cover. "Uh, *Shakespeare in Love*." He was caught.

"Ah," said his friend meaningfully.

"Yeah. Chick flick. Girlfriend wants to see it," Brian said, laughing awkwardly.

"Right," said his friend, smiling a bit smugly. "Well, see you around."

The same battle is played out in any number of recent films. For example, in *You've Got Mail*, Tom Hanks plays a Jekyll/Hyde character, torn between being a ruthless businessman and a sensitive listener. I saw the film first on television, where it was broadcast as part of the local network's series of *Flicks for Chicks and Sensitive Guys*. In the commercial breaks, they advertised their Thursday night series, *Guys' Night In*, where the movies feature car crashes and oversized guns. The implication is clear: when guys get together and away from the girls, they can indulge in their true pleasures. It's all a bit tongue-in-cheek, but it's also pretty shrewd marketing.

Individual boys buy in to the dominant mythology in differing degrees, shuffling elements to fit with other aspects of their local (family, school, neighborhood, ethnic) cultures, continuously working to construct a version of masculinity that they can live with. To the extent that they buy in to the dominant stereotypes, they may well have problems with school English, because it's about reading books and writing and reflecting about inner experience. It's an educational cliché to think that weak students suffer poor self-esteem, but there's more than one kind of self-esteem. High self-esteem *as a guy* may seem incompatible with doing well in English (Skelton 2001, 103).

Who Buys in to Dominant Masculinity?

Can we quantify the extent to which boys do buy in to this ideology? Probably not really, but one large research project has produced data that I find interesting.

The purpose of the project was to examine the self-images of a thousand boys and girls, ages twelve to eighteen. A team of psychologists wanted to follow up the claim that girls were being silenced in adolescence, that they were losing a sense of authentic self and voice. That line of thought had been advanced most famously by Carol Gilligan in her book *In a Different Voice* (1982) and by Mary Pipher in *Reviving Ophelia* (1994), but there hadn't been any systematic research to examine whether girls actually lost the ability to speak their minds any *more* than boys did.

These researchers found that comfort to voice one's thoughts varied quite a bit depending on the situation and relationship, as one would expect. (For many, it's easier to speak to a small group of friends than it is to address a large classroom, for example.) There didn't turn out to be huge differences between boys and girls, nor did most girls in this study appear to be troubled by lack of voice (Harter, Waters, and Whitesell 1997, 161–62). It may be, of course, that several decades of the women's movement have resulted in girls feeling more confident by the end of the 1990s than the girls Gilligan was writing about in the early 1980s.

What I find most interesting is another aspect of the study. The subjects all completed a personality questionnaire that assessed the degree to which individuals bought in to stereotypes of masculine or feminine attitudes. They were asked to rate the extent to which they would want to develop personal qualities like "sensitivity," "enjoyment of babies," "gentleness," "independence," "risk taking," "athleticism," and so on—

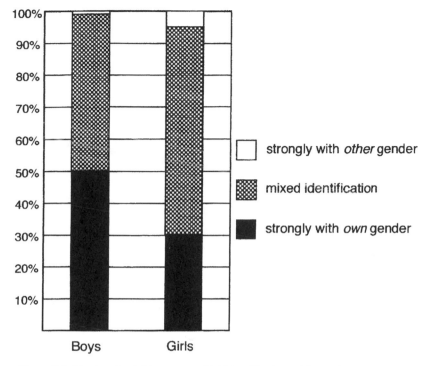

Figure 2.1 Twelve- to eighteen-year-olds' identification with gender stereotypes (Data derived from Harter, Waters, and Whitesell 1997)

a list deliberately chosen to include stereotypical masculine and feminine qualities. The results can be seen in Figure 2.1.

One striking feature of this data is the fact that, compared to girls, a significantly larger group of boys holds on to traditional notions of appropriate gender roles. Around 65 percent to 75 percent—in other words, *most*—girls are prepared to identify with a wide range of human qualities, embracing both the traditionally masculine and the traditionally feminine. This may be a credit to the women's movement, which has been telling girls that it is possible to be gentle *and* forceful, a listener *and* a leader. This represents an opening up of possibilities for those girls, but boys don't seem to have gone as far down that road: *fully half the boys reported strong identification with traditional masculine stereotypes*. Of course, as I mentioned in Chapter 1, boys haven't had the motivation to change: when you think you're at the top of the pile, it's not so easy to see why you would want to take on traits of those lower in the hierarchy.

Incidentally, in terms of voice—the ability to express one's thoughts openly—some problems arose for the subjects who had the strongest identification with the stereotypes of their own sex. Ultrafeminine girls reported the least confident voices in public situations like the classroom (163); ultramasculine boys were unlikely to speak intimately with their close male friends (164).

A study like this makes it clear that we need to separate the concepts of *sex* and *gender*, if we take *gender* to include an understanding of how one performs the role of a boy or girl and what practices are appropriate. All the students in this research are biologically of one *sex* or the other, but their sense of *gender* identification varies widely. There's a whole range of gender styles on offer out there in the social, cultural marketplace, although it seems that girls have fewer constraints on which attitudes they can adopt.

If we agree that willingness to engage in literacy activities is connected with gender identification, a few important principles follow logically.

First, we realize that we're not just talking about problems that only boys have in English. Lots of girls evidently endorse some masculine ideals. The particular mix of values will be different from girl to girl, and it would be nice if they embraced only the finest stereotypes of masculinity—athleticism, leadership, and so forth—but, in truth, we know that some girls pick up less admirable masculine traits. Smoking, membership in violent girl gangs, and other risk-taking behaviors are on the rise among teenage girls. As girls configure for themselves identities that include hitherto masculine traits, some of them inevitably pick up some of the antireading, anti-English attitudes that are implied by dominant masculinity.

And this is true, isn't it? We all know there are some girls who don't like English, who don't like reading books or writing their thoughts down. There are girls who feel more comfortable in the science lab than in the English classroom, just as there are guys (like me) who feel more comfortable with books than with test tubes.

In other words, when I talk about *boys* in this book, please understand that what I usually really mean is *a certain subset of students that has difficulty valuing and succeeding in the subject English*—a group that includes some but not all boys, and certainly includes some girls as well. I think you probably don't want me to have to keep repeating that whole mouthful, so you'll forgive me if, from now on, I just say *boys* and expect you to understand that I don't mean all boys; I mean instead that special group I've just defined.

As a result, here are two principles to keep in mind.

We must be skeptical of any program that treats all boys (or all girls) as if they were all the same. Many different things are going on inside individual boys and girls. If you decide you're going to take all the boys into a separate room and give them a special version of Boys-Only English, it will be wrong for some boys. (It would have been wrong for me.) If all boys start kindergarten one year later to allow time to catch up on literacy, it will be wrong for some boys. (It would have been wrong for my son.) Such segregation will also be a disservice to the many girls who would have benefited from exactly the same measures that are applied to the boys.

We must be prepared for the likelihood that strategies intended to help boys will also benefit many girls. That means that, in the short run, closing the gap between the scores of boys and girls can't be the only measure of success. It may well turn out that a good literacy program raises boys' scores *and* raises girls' average scores too, so that a gap may persist. In Britain, where a number of schools have made concentrated efforts to improve boys' work in English (using approaches like the ones I will describe in the rest of this book), the achievement gap sometimes narrows, but sometimes the average marks of both sexes go up. (See, for example, Penny 1998, 103.) We have to accept that helping lots of students—both boys and girls—is more important than fixing statistics.

I'm convinced that when future historians look back on our era, they will see the period since about 1965 as a time of great upheaval in gender identities. Women have moved into positions formerly denied to them, men are being challenged to reconsider their traditional roles, and the status of homosexuality has been radically reassessed. Popular culture shows our fascination with dissolving gender boundaries, as seen in movies like *Mrs. Doubtfire*, *The Crying Game*, and *Boys Don't Cry* and in androgynous performers like David Bowie, Michael Jackson, and Marilyn Manson. The time of upheaval isn't over yet.

Our subject, English, can't avoid being caught up in this storm. English is about literate practices that have been identified, in some boys' minds, with women. In a world where being an "able-bodied man" is no longer a satisfactory qualification for employment, that identification has to be broken. That means changing boys' minds a bit, and it means changing the subject a bit. When girls were invited to think of themselves as being mathematicians, doors opened for them. Our boys need to have doors opened for them as well. This isn't about social engineering, or trying to feminize boys. It's about helping all our students see that there are many ways to be men and women, and that the kind of literacy and culture offered by the English classroom has a place in a man's life just as much as in a woman's life.

3 Classroom Visit

Grade 11, Nonacademic

I have found it useful occasionally to step out of my own classroom and watch fellow teachers at work with their students. Freed from the necessity to think on my feet, I see things that I might not have noticed if I were the teacher myself. I share those observations here in the chapters called "Classroom Visits." Sometimes I can't resist suggesting something else that the teacher might have done, but for the most part I try not to second-guess the colleagues who generously allowed me to bring my notepad to their lessons. It's easy for anyone, sitting quietly away from the whirl of the classroom, to reflect on what might have been, but thrown into the pressure of school life, any of us might have done the same as these teachers. The real value of these visits lies in the opportunity just to watch boys and girls in English classrooms. The teachers and students are all identified by pseudonyms, but the stories are all true.

There are twenty names on Joan Dodgson's grade 11 class list—fourteen boys and six girls—but actual attendance varies widely from day to day. The course is labeled "general level," which means that students signing up for it know they won't be going to university. Some may hope to earn a diploma from a community college; others plan to go straight to work after high school. Whatever their plans, the attrition rate is high: six students have already withdrawn and more will disappear throughout the year. Because grade 11 English is a compulsory credit, dropping this course probably means quitting school. At the midpoint of the term, the class average was below a passing mark.

Joan worries about this class, and especially about the boys. Their lack of interest, their disastrous achievement, and their frequent personal crises are emotionally wearing on Joan, who is a caring and earnest teacher. In September, the boys were frankly hostile and abrupt in their treatment of her. The tension has been easing lately, but she still feels she has to brace herself for each encounter. She is understandably anxious about allowing an observer into her room, since she can never be sure what will happen from day to day. "I go in with a lesson to teach," she says, "but then there are all these other issues that have to be taken care of."

I sit in a back corner and watch students file in. In classrooms where students choose their own seats, I am used to seeing distinct girls and boys sections of the room, but this class is one of the most strikingly segregated I have ever seen. Five of the six girls huddle together in a cluster on one side of the room, no empty seats between them. The boys, in contrast, are diffused throughout the rest of the room. There is enough furniture that most of the boys are able to have an empty desk on at least one side, so that they can turn around and stretch out an arm or a leg. Visually, the impression is that the girls are a tight group, taking up the least possible room, while the boys are a scattering of individuals, spreading out comfortably to fill all the available space.

Some of the boys wear heavy winter coats, which they do not remove. Staying in coats happens fairly frequently among general-level boys at all the schools I've taught at, although some teachers make a rule against it. Is this a way for boys to make themselves look bigger, hiding their slim adolescent bodies? Is the outerwear an extra protective layer? (Some students would, if you let them, bury their heads inside jacket hoods.) Is it an unconscious signal that they're only passing through this room, not really planning to stay? Or are they more poorly nourished and therefore genuinely cold? (General-level students sometimes complain that a room is chilly; I've seen a class of academic students come into the same room a few minutes later and ask to cool the room by opening windows.) But if that's the case, why do so many of them wear only a summer T-shirt under the coat?

Aside from the small island of girls, there is one other girl in the class, who has isolated herself in a back corner, far from the other girls, beside a window. In a class so clearly divided along sex lines, her differentness is conspicuous. She is the only girl who wears a hat and winter coat through the lesson. Her seating and clothing align her with the boys; socially, however, she seems disconnected from everyone else in the room. (Later, Joan describes her as a bright girl who does not hand work in and will probably fail.)

Four boys arrive throughout the lesson, noticeably late. No girls are late.

The day before, these students had been out of school on a job-shadowing assignment, spending the day with someone in a career that interests them. Today Joan starts by inviting anyone to share brief thoughts about yesterday's experience. Sam is eager to tell us that he had been with a photojournalist who took a picture of a hockey referee who had been hit in the face by a puck. The picture is on the front page of today's newspaper, which Sam holds up for us to see. Other boys comment on this admiringly. They like the picture, with "tough guy" appreciation for the damage that had been done to the referee's face: "Yeah, he got his face mashed up good!" (Joan tells me that sports injuries and fights are popular topics for these boys.)

At this point, Eric arrives. I know Eric: I taught him when he was in grade 9 several years back. He is athletically built and has always seemed friendly but has had a troubled history in and out of school and should have graduated long ago. He tells Joan that he is late because he is suffering back pain and was trying to get the front office to allow him to sign out and go home. Instead, they have sent him back to class. (This probably means that a poor attendance record has made the office staff doubt his excuses. They wouldn't have been able to contact a parent because Eric lives on his own.) Joan expresses concern and we learn that a nerve in Eric's back is pinched as the result of a football injury. Joan doesn't doubt the sincerity of his story, and neither do I. The boys also show their concern. Tactfully, they don't *say* anything—boys often don't—but the attentive turn of their heads shows their respect for Eric's condition. I notice the difference between their almost sadistic pleasure in the news story of the injured referee and their decent silence, just a few minutes later, in the immediacy of a classmate's pain. Joan allows Eric to sit on a table at the side of the room, rather than trying to bend his large, hurting body into a student's desk.

The main part of the lesson now begins. They are reading Salinger's *Catcher in the Rye*. Joan says, "Now, where are we? Oh, yes. We're doing Chapter 16 today. It's one of my favorites." I'm sitting at the back and Kevin, beside me, who has been quiet to this point, mutters sarcastically to himself, "Oh yeah. It's one of my favorites, too." Kevin has home problems, drinking problems, and school problems, and he may well not graduate. I think about his sarcasm. Here's a teacher—a woman, and maybe that matters—standing up and saying she has favorite bits of books, and here's a kid who is quietly contemptuous, even irritated by her attitude. I don't want to overinterpret his throwaway comment, but it's as if he's saying, "You wouldn't catch *me* admitting anything like that in public."

Joan asks for a summary of the chapter and, for the first time, a girl speaks. She gives a correct answer, in what turns out to be the characteristic pattern of girls' speech in this class. Girls' comments are rare and are always framed as answers to specific, text-based questions posed by the teacher. The interchange with girls has a recitative quality. ("How does Holden feel about . . . ?" answered by "He feels that . . .") They wait for the teacher to ask a question, raise their hands, and wait for the teacher to acknowledge them. Their responses are safe: they know that they know the answer. The boys, on the other hand, are much more likely to interject spontaneous comments that are only loosely, if at all, tied to the book. In fact, it's clear that many of them haven't read the chapter.

Joan wants to teach the concept of *empathy*. This is an interesting project, because women reportedly experience empathy more easily than men do. If that's true, it might explain why girls do a better job of answering questions requiring them to understand the motivations of a character (Head 1999, 69). Joan writes the word *empathy* on the blackboard and tells the students to copy it into their notes. A few do; most don't. After explaining what it means, she asks, "Have you ever been in a situation where you felt empathy?"

There is a thoughtful pause, and then Eric, in a tone that lies somewhere between puzzlement and amazement, says, "Well, *sure*. Everyone does." His surprise, if I'm reading it correctly, seems to be at the idea of even having to ask such a question: of *course* people feel empathy! Frank, another student whom I know and who has been a "problem" for years, tells us a story about his brother trashing their shared room because he was so angry at their father. Frank describes a mix of feelings: he was angry at his brother for wrecking the room, but also understood what it was like to be this furious and felt sorry for him, knowing that his brother would regret what he had done. It was a quick, articulate sketch of mixed feelings from a boy that many teachers, over the years, have seen as an uncooperative lout.

For me, this is an interesting moment. Eric and Frank have suffered lots of failure in school and are both considerably older than normal for grade 11. There are a couple of other boys in the same situation and, as the lesson goes on, this older cohort shows the most willingness to engage in the discussion of feelings the teacher obviously wants. Boys who are closer to the right age for the class—about sixteen years—are attentive enough, but they don't offer to join the conversation. I wonder if it is simply a question of time necessary for maturing. The older boys—they're maybe eighteen, nineteen years old—show decency and depth that I never saw when I taught them years earlier. If understanding feelings is one of the things we want from English, there's hope for all these boys as they grow older. The younger ones may be wary of joining in, but they are listening and it's good for them to hear their older peers, not just the teacher, talking like this. Not every class will have older, well-liked students like Eric and Frank to set an example, and this discussion might well have hit a roadblock if there were only the younger boys in the room, but at least the *capacity* is there. Unlocking it is the challenge.

I'm also interested by the puzzled surprise in Eric's response, the feeling that the teacher was asking a question almost too obvious to answer:

"Have you ever felt empathy?" "Of course. How could you even ask?" I hear the same tone later in the lesson when Joan asks about the child that Holden sees: "Why is this child happy?" After a couple of seconds, one of the older boys bursts out, "Because it's a *child*," as if he wonders, "Why does she keep asking these questions? Doesn't she understand?" With prodding, he goes on to explain about childhood's innocence, but it's clear that he figures everyone ought to know this already. For the teacher, of course, articulating this understanding of life and bringing it to bear on Salinger's novel is exactly what needs to be done. As English teachers, our assumption is sometimes that things have to be spoken or written to be real. It's the right assumption for our subject, but it's not the automatic assumption for all our students. For some of them, our insistence that they talk about thoughts and feelings is puzzling, just as some husbands feel puzzled or irritated by partners who keep asking them what they're thinking, what they're feeling.

In Eric's response, there may also be a problem with a too-literal understanding of the question. Joan asked, "Have you ever been in a situation where you felt empathy?" Taken at its literal level, the answer *has* to be "yes," unless the person is a callous monster. In other words, to a literal mind, the question may have a threatening edge, like the stereotyped scenario in which a frustrated woman asks a man, "Don't you have any feelings at all?" You and I know that Joan didn't mean to put into question whether her students had ever in their whole lives shared anyone's feelings. Rather, she meant to invite a short discussion of such experiences—a difficult enough task itself for reticent students, but not nearly as odd as the literal question. You may well protest, "But who would take such a question literally?" His response suggests that Eric did, for one. According to linguists like Deborah Tannen, in *You Just Don't Understand*, focusing on the literal message is exactly what men are more likely to do (1990, 174–76).

In later chapters, bringing boys into the patterns of talk and thought that are typical of our subject will be my main theme. Here, I'll just suggest a simple rewording that might have made a difference. Instead of asking whether people have ever felt empathy, I wonder what would have happened if Joan had started by claiming common feelings. After defining *empathy*, she might have said, "I think we've all had the experience of knowing what someone else was feeling—feeling *with* him or her. Could someone give us an example of that, just to make sure we're all talking about the same thing?" That wording wouldn't solve all the problems attached to classroom talk about feelings, but it would at least send the right message to the literal-minded.

Throughout the lesson, Joan works hard to help students get at the emotional quality of *Catcher in the Rye*. I know she feels frustrated by what sometimes seems a lack of response, but when she pushes them to think about Holden's personal qualities and relationships, I see subtle signs of interest from these boys. Many of them don't say much, but when there is talk about how people treat each other, their attention does not wander. Their eyes are glued on the speaker, whether it be Joan or one of the other students. I watch one boy who sits through the whole class with his books closed, arms folded tightly across his chest, face unexpressive, until at one point Joan says, "Holden is lucky to have a loving family," and then this boy nods thoughtfully. It's almost the only response I see from him all period, but who is to say this lesson had no impact on him? We had better not confuse lack of verbal response with lack of interest.

There is a reference to *Hamlet* at one point in the novel. Of course, these kids know nothing about *Hamlet*, and it would be easy enough for Joan to sidestep the allusion, but she wants them to know something about literature, so she quickly summarizes Shakespeare's plot. Students, especially the boys, are visibly engaged by this retelling. *Hamlet* is a great story, after all, full of sex, murder, and intrigue. When she tells them about Gertrude's quick remarriage, some of the boys are literally on the edge of their seats: "Miss, isn't that pretty *bad*?!" Joan counters with, "How do you feel about what his mother has done?" and someone calls out, "It's *disgusting*!" (Again, the little hint of astonishment that she'd have to ask such a question.) They can't wait to get on with the story: "So does he go and bust up his uncle?" When they find out that Hamlet does not immediately "bust up" his uncle, they are outraged—"Oh Miss!" "That's awful!" "He's a wuss!"—but later reassured to learn of the final blood-bath. (Joan tells me they also call Holden Caulfield a wuss because he doesn't want to fight.)

In this little episode we see stereotypical macho attitudes in the taste for blood and revenge, but what I also see is that these kids, who are at risk, underachieving, and definitely don't like English, can get completely wrapped up in a story, can feel strongly about fictional characters and care about their fates. Some people say that such students should have an education geared much more to "functional" literacy and the practical demands of the workplace, but when I see the way these boys are galvanized by the simple plot summary of *Hamlet*, I think we must somehow be on the right track (or, at least, at the right station) in choosing stories as our subject matter.

Throughout this, Kevin, the boy beside me who had been sarcastic about having "favorite" chapters of a book, remains impassive. Joan now explains that Holden's reference to *Hamlet* is called an *allusion*. She writes the word on the blackboard and defines it. When he hears the definition, Kevin mutters in disgust, *"Jeez!"* I think the idea of books referring to other books has pushed him to exasperation. Of course, TV shows like

The Simpsons and popular songs regularly make references to other cultural objects, and maybe starting with examples from popular culture would have been, for Kevin, a more palatable introduction to the idea of allusion.

Class is at an end for today, and as Kevin packs up his books (which, as a matter of fact, have never been opened), he shakes his head incredulously. I can't tell whether he's irritated more by the things books do or by the things English teachers do.

When I return the next day, Joan is checking homework. It appears that only four kids have done a satisfactory job: two girls and two boys. Deciding to confront the class about this homework record, Joan says, "Put yourself in my shoes. When I see that most of you aren't doing your homework, what am I supposed to think?" I note that this fits conveniently with yesterday's theme of thinking about how other people feel, and the boys—only the boys—cheerfully call out possible things that she might think, although I'm not sure they've gone very far in empathizing with their teacher.

"That we're lazy?"

"That we didn't have time?"

"That it's too hard?"

"It's just that I had a bad week?"

Joan sighs and moves on with today's lesson. She wants to get them thinking about setting and asks them to recall any time they could remember seeing a beautiful place. They look blank, so she tells them about seeing the countryside colored by autumn leaves and how that moved her.

This seems to jog Peter, who offers a related memory: "Yeah, my cottage, because there are no worries there."

Determined to make the most of this offering, Joan tries to get Peter to describe that scene, but he doesn't have a command of descriptive language, so Joan has to feed him his lines.

"Are there trees?"

"Yeah."

"What about water? Is there water, a lake?"

"Yeah."

"What do you see when you're there?" Silence. "Can you see the other side?"

"Yeah."

"What does the water look like?" Silence. "Is it calm or is it choppy?"

"Calm."

Peter isn't being resistant. He looks absorbed in his memories. He is, I am sure, genuinely seeing that cottage in his own mind, and I believe he wants to tell the teacher what he sees, but he doesn't know what he is supposed to say. There are *categories* of description that a more verbal person would use as scaffolding for building a picture: you could talk, for example, about different impressions through the five senses, or about trees/wildlife/weather/landforms, about different kinds of activities at the cottage, about the atmosphere at different times of the day, and so on. Most of that scaffolding, that knowledge of categories, may be missing, however, in a relatively nonverbal teenager like Peter.

A mother of a teenage son and daughter told me that when her daughter comes home from a concert, she's bursting to share the sights and sounds of the event. However, if the mother asks the son how the concert was, he'll grunt, "Yeah, it was good." Maybe he doesn't want to talk—that's a real possibility—but it's also possible that he honestly doesn't know what to say. In later chapters, we'll talk about the ways we can help build the scaffolding that will help students find words.

As Joan continues, she introduces a new concept. "Have you heard the word *utopia*?"

A boy calls out, "*Fruitopia*? Isn't that a drink?" The class laughs.

Joan calls upon a girl with her hand up, who gives the correct answer: "It means a perfect world."

The boy has made a bid for attention by calling out an answer that seems irrelevant, intended as a joke, while the girl has been polite and correct. But you know, Fruitopia actually isn't irrelevant: the student has made a quick connection with the name of a drink sold in the cafeteria, and that brand name is in fact a play on the word *utopia*. The teacher could have used that to teach the idea of utopia. However, if she had *at that moment* talked about Fruitopia, she might have never gotten to the girl who was respecting the school convention of raising one's hand. That would send a message that impulsive calling out by a boy wins the teacher's attention more effectively than appropriate behavior by a girl. That would be exactly the kind of unfairness that Myra and David Sadker wrote about in *Failing at Fairness* (1994), their influential study of how girls are "cheated" by schools.

Still, by ignoring the boy's outburst, Joan has missed a teachable moment. The student did a good thing: he didn't know what *utopia* meant, but the word triggered an association that he was prepared to pay attention to. This is thinking we want to encourage, but because he doesn't have much confidence in his own thinking, the boy dismisses the thought as a joke. We would be doing him a favor if we were to grab his thinking and show him how to turn it into something more constructive.

After honoring the girl's correct answer, we could turn back to that boy and question his thinking. We might have said something like this: "Jim, you called out *Fruitopia*, because it sounded like *utopia*. You thought that was just a joke, didn't you? But actually you're on to something there. Now that you've heard Vanessa tell us what the word really means, what do you think might be the reason for that brand name?" The long-term goal is to get Jim to honor his own thinking, so that he begins to see himself as a thoughtful participant in the class, not just as a joker. (We'll come back to jokers in the next chapter.)

As today's class goes on, the discussion turns to alienation, and Joan tells her students that the rates of depression and suicide rise during the Christmas season. This seems to strike a chord, and there is a sudden flurry of calling out from the boys.

"Yeah, because if your life stinks . . . ," begins Eric.

"But that's not everyone. You're talking about bums," interrupts someone else.

"They'd have to have low self-esteem," says a third boy.

This gets a laugh from several people, and Eric snorts. "*Self-esteem?* Where'd you get that word from?" It's interesting that Eric, who, in his initial comment, seems to be on the teacher's wavelength concerning holiday depression, mocks a student for apparently trying to use impressive vocabulary. These kids are prepared to enter into straight talk about life issues but are on guard against any of their peers using language that smells of school or books. This is a problem for teachers. We probably don't think the term *self-esteem* is terribly pretentious, and we'd like to see our students gain control over language that will win them entry into the rewards of further education and careers. However, some peer groups create an insidious culture that warns kids against breaking ranks and going over to "the other side," that is, to the school side. Sometimes when that kind of language comes up in class, we have to be prepared to defend its users, declaring our support, not because the language is impressive, fancy, or intelligent sounding, but because it's useful.

Later, discussion turns to museums, suggested by the museum in *Catcher in the Rye*. Joan asks if anyone has visited a museum. Many of these students have been on school trips to the Royal Ontario Museum in Toronto. Joan asks what they remember, and there are calls from around the room.

"The dinosaurs."

"The weapons."

"The mummies."

"Oh yeah! Remember that dead child. . . ."

There's suddenly talk all over the room. It's a strange moment, as almost everyone seems to come alive with nostalgia, chattering about this place that so many have visited in their childhoods.

The class' conversation has a life of its own. Lots of kids, boys and girls, spontaneously take turns, for the moment not needing the teacher's management. They get going on the nature of historical knowledge, as one boy asks, "When they show 'a day in the life' of someone who lived five thousand years ago, like really, how do they know?"

Another boy answers, "Someone's grandma tells someone else, and they tell someone, blah blah blah."

Joan offers, "That's called the oral tradition."

A student muses aloud, "*Art . . . ? Articles?* What do you call them? *Artifacts.*"

"But I bet they're making a lot of it up."

Joan turns to the boy who said that, and asks, "Is that what you think when your history teacher tells you stuff?"

Several voices answer emphatically in unison, "*YES!*" (It's not everyone who joins that chorus, but I catch a glimpse of just how deeply runs the suspicion of school and book learning for at least some of them.)

This all leads naturally to consideration of the importance of memory. Joan asks why the museum is so important to Holden.

"Because it's the one thing that hasn't changed," comes back the answer firmly from Eric.

Joan tells a story about her own pleasure in walking past her childhood home, because of the memories it holds. She asks if they can remember such a place, and I realize that the whole class is now sitting up, alert, thinking, feeling. They seem somehow touched by this evocation of their memories, in a way that I think is relevant to Holden's feelings about the museum. Even Kevin, the withdrawn skeptic beside me, leans forward and listens as the outsider girl—the one who sits apart from the enclave of the other girls—haltingly, musingly describes her grandmother's house and what it means to her. She finishes and asks permission to use the washroom.

The last ten minutes are for students to read ahead in *Catcher* or work on their notes. I don't think much work is done. The girls, silent for most of the class, come alive, whispering and giggling. The boys stretch out and occasionally question each other about their weekend plans. Joan quietly approaches Kevin, who sits beside me, staring into space.

"Kevin, are you reading?"

"Yeah, I am." He turns his eyes to his novel, and for the next two minutes he does appear to read. (I time him.) Then he closes his book and waits for the end of the period.

Teaching this class is tiring and frustrating for Joan. She is moving through *Catcher in the Rye* at a maddeningly slow pace. Homework usually isn't completed. She can't count on the class' goodwill toward the subject. The boys especially have often seemed to threaten Joan's vision of what the subject ought to be. Many—too many—will fail at the end of the semester. Some (like Eric) will be asked to leave school before the end of the year.

Still, as an outsider visiting this difficult class, I am struck by what *is* happening sometimes. Not all the time, but sometimes, the life inside these students is being touched—visibly *stirred*—by a teacher who has not given up on them. For Joan, Salinger's novel is about the world inside people and the importance of caring for that inner world. She is relentlessly, even heroically, pursuing that vision with her students. She is not achieving enough to satisfy her, but it is something.

As her students shuffle out of class, I think about the important work Joan is trying to do with these kids. I am moved by the reflection and surprised to find tears welling up in my eyes. I'm glad it's lunchtime, because that means there won't be another class crowding into the room. Man that I am, I wouldn't want them to see my tears, would I?

4 *Wuss!*

Dealing with Feelings

Some weeks after the classroom visits described in Chapter 3, Joan Dodgson told me that one day Eric asked to be excused to sit outside in the hall. Joan sensed that the best thing was to agree to his request without further question. At an appropriate break in her lesson, she slipped out to the hall and found Eric awash in tears.

It turned out that Eric and his girlfriend had broken up on the weekend. The girl in question was a student in our school, and today she wasn't speaking to Eric in the halls. Eric couldn't count on support from home, because he didn't live there anymore. (He had earlier explained to Joan, "My mom's a single mom with two little kids to take care of. She doesn't need me to take care of, too.")

As Joan and Eric talked, he carefully turned away from students passing in the hall. Joan realized that Eric had two problems that day. One was the traumatic break-up. The other was the shameful discovery that he couldn't control his feelings.

"Miss, look at me crying like a girl," he wept. "I'm a wuss. I'm a girl, Miss." In this condition, he didn't know how he could continue through the day.

Joan looked at this big, strong, football player and did her best to tell him that he wasn't a "girl": he was a sensitive boy who was hurting because he had lost a relationship that mattered to him. She told him it made sense to feel bad and that anyone who had lost someone he or she cared about ought to feel the same.

Joan tried to mirror Eric's feelings back to him in a way that would tell him that his emotions and his expressions of those emotions were understandable and honorable. Eric's heart was broken and he wasn't likely to learn many school lessons that morning, but maybe he could learn something about accepting his emotional life.

It is common to contrast male reticence with female willingness to talk about feelings. Often this is explained by women's desire to achieve rapport: revealing something of yourself has a payoff in the interdependent connections that are built with your listeners. For men, rapport—so the theory goes—isn't as important as establishing independent status in a social network that is structured more by hierarchy than by interdependence. Talking about sports, politics, computers, or some other factually based topic allows men to show off knowledge without risking personal vulnerability (Tannen 1990, 92). The truth probably isn't quite as simple as that popular explanation. After all, men do desire and achieve connection—the famous male bonding—although it may be through different means than women would choose, and women do have ways of signaling status and preserving their independence.

Still, this explanation probably has some truth and can help us begin to understand the special flavor of shame that can come from a boy's exhibition of softer emotions. For boys, to a certain extent, social relationships are about finding your place on a ladder; revealing your weakness moves you a step down that ladder. Anger, fierce loyalty, righteous indignation—those kinds of feelings are acceptable because they fit the image of the tough warrior, ready to fight to defend the honor of his country, his gang, his girl, or his own name. (On the other hand, there is also a cool, detached version of masculinity that has contempt for even those hot emotions.) The soft emotions, however, are women's, and as long as masculinity is defined negatively, as "not feminine," then the boy who displays such feelings in public risks shame. As William Pollack writes in *Real Boys*, "While girls may be shame-sensitive, boys are shame-*phobic*: they are exquisitely yet unconsciously attuned to any signal of 'loss of face' and will do just about whatever it takes to avoid shame" (1998, 33).

In this chapter, I'm going to talk about how emotions can be handled in the English classroom, but before I turn to practical suggestions, I begin by acknowledging the emotional life of boys. Then I'll address the special problem of the classroom joker, who declines intellectual or emotional involvement, and finally I'll turn to basic strategies for handling the emotional content of the subject English.

A Reminder: Boys Have Feelings Too

The line of thought outlined earlier, you'll notice, assumes that boys do have a range of feelings; it's just that there's a cultural expectation—what Pollack calls the "Boy Code"—that renders expression of those feelings inappropriate. It may seem too obvious to insist that, yes, boys have feelings too, but I think some of us slip into the dangerous idea that boys don't have feelings, that emotions are the special province of girls and women.

You've heard it, I'm sure. You've heard women saying, "Men! They're just so insensitive. They don't seem to have any feelings." Or you've heard men saying, "Those women keep getting bogged down in their emotions," as if that never happens to men. The stereotype of the un-feeling male is partly a consequence of the macho ideal of toughness being taken at face value. It is also the legacy of an intellectual history that, in earlier generations, made Reason and Emotion square off against each other; Reason aligned with men and Emotion with women.

In *You Just Don't Understand*, Deborah Tannen reports on an interest-ing experiment in which male pairs and female pairs were each asked to talk about "something serious." The partners in each conversation were previously known to each other, and the conversations videotaped and analyzed. Grade 6 girls seemed comfortable talking about "friends, friend-ship, and feelings" with "subtlety and complexity" that were not found in their male counterparts. Grade 6 boys had difficulty sitting still and flitted from topic to topic, seldom mentioning friends or relationships (1990, 265).

Most interesting, however, are the grade 10 conversations. Girls pulled their chairs together and looked into each other's eyes, while a pair of boys sat parallel to each other, looking straight ahead, as if each was forbidden to look at the other. Physically, they seemed detached, but surprisingly they actually talked with great intimacy about their relation-ship and their troubled feelings (266). In fact, closer examination of their parallel seating showed that they were so attentive to each other that they echoed each other's postures.

> *Their motions are finely coordinated. They make similar movements, in similar directions, at the same time. They are acting in concert, . . . like two geese preening their feathers, seeming to ignore each other but mir-roring each other's movements in coordinated rhythm.* (269)

There are two important lessons for us here. First, we should note that boys may well have a different physical style of intimacy. Some of our usual assumptions about the importance of facing the speaker and mak-ing eye contact may work well for women, but may be threatening for boys who, at moments of revelation, particularly with other boys, may need to deflect attention and direct their gaze to some other object. That has implications for how we deal with boys and how we expect them to deal with each other in paired or small-group work. Side-by-side collabo-ration may be easier than head-on meetings.

The second lesson, of course, is that boys do have feelings and can talk about them. This grade 10 conversation was admittedly unusual and there's no doubt that it's normally easier for boys to fall back on joking, friendly taunting, and swapping information about sports or cars, but their feelings are real too, and there are ways of talking about them. In fact, when talking with women and girls rather than other men, boys sometimes seem quite willing and able to express feelings, perhaps since they aren't in the same competitive relationship with women as they are with men (Maccoby 1998, 200–01). I began this chapter with the story about Eric confiding in a female teacher; he may not have been as likely to reveal feelings to a male teacher.

Contrary to the myth of women's greater emotionality, there is evidence that in the case of negative feelings, men actually have more intense emotional responses. In *Emotional Intelligence*, Daniel Goleman notes that men are susceptible to "flooding," or being taken over by negative emotions, at lower thresholds of negativity than women. This results in an increased flow of adrenaline into the bloodstream and it takes men longer than women to recover from this overwhelming experience. It has been suggested that men stonewall to protect themselves from flooding, because becoming silent and stoic does in fact lower the heart rate (1995, 140). Of course, stonewalling has the adverse consequence of irritating women in the man's life, and in the long term, chronically repressed anger or fear has debilitating consequences for one's mental and physical health.

In *Raising Cain*, Kindlon and Thompson report on an experiment in which a tape of a baby crying was played to second-grade boys and girls, whose reactions were monitored. Interestingly, boys were *more* upset than girls by the sound of the infant's distress, although girls were more likely to do something useful to calm the baby. (An adult had told them they could talk to the baby over a speaker.) The boys resorted to flipping a switch that would simply turn off the monitor.

> *The researchers theorized that children—in this case, boys—who are more easily stressed by emotional responses may prefer to avoid them. In other words, boys who have trouble managing their own emotions may routinely tune out the cues of other people's upset. (1999, 11)*

Let us agree, then, that boys have feelings—indeed, intense feelings. After all, when any group has an unusually high incidence of suicide, as teenage boys do, it's not a sign of lack of feeling. They may handle those feelings differently than girls, they may not handle them well, they may be ashamed of their feelings and try to block them out, and it may well be that their feelings aren't always aroused by books. But they do have feelings.

Engaging the Joker

It has been observed that men's talk often seems to be "a form of display, involving joke telling, boasting, ribbing, and verbal aggression" (Corson 2001, 160). Young men's friendship groups may spend a lot of time joking around. Often baffling or tiresome to women, this behavior helps establish a pecking order, as each participant competes to come up with a cleverer line than the last speaker. It's also a bonding ritual, as the boys prove to each other that they're all good guys, the sort of people with whom you can have a laugh. A boy who can't summon up this kind of wit risks being branded as boring.

Sometimes this all stays outside the classroom, but sometimes it doesn't. Class clowns are almost always boys, sometimes boys who have not developed physically as quickly as their classmates. Physical size is a demonstration of masculinity, and the boy who is thinner or shorter than the rest, or noticeably overweight, may turn to clowning as a way of defining a role for himself (Newberger 1999, 208). I vividly remember Rahim, a boy so short he was receiving hormone treatments, who loved to get a laugh with provocative, outlandish comments in class. When we read Shakespeare's *Twelfth Night* aloud, he begged every day to play the part of Feste the Fool, and we all recognized his special affinity for the role of the jester.

Sometimes the luck of the draw delivers a pack of jokers into the same room, and their clowning threatens to hijack the teacher's agenda. It can be devastating for the emotional content of the course. I've heard plenty of frustrated teachers complaining, "The boys in that class make it impossible to do the really good stuff. Every time the discussion shows any hint of going somewhere serious, someone makes a stupid joke, and then everyone's laughing and we've lost the moment." The nature of English is such that we do want to talk about things that are important or serious, but the nature of these boys is to veer away from such talk. In part, they have to dissociate themselves from the discussion to prove that they're "one of the guys"; also, they may not trust their own ability to participate in serious discussion without embarrassing themselves.

The jokers can be a serious challenge for the English teacher. If we let the banter go on, we may be surrendering the opportunity for reflection, which is a loss for the jokers and for all the other kids in the class. If we try to smother the joking with pursed lips and a wet blanket of discipline, we risk becoming a parody of the English teacher: all solemn high-mindedness and correct grammar, but no joy or spontaneity.

The unwelcome joke that arises in the classroom may deliver three messages. First, it says, "I'm clever. See how fast my mind works." Second, it says, "I'm not doing the serious business of this class; I'm redirecting the conversation down a blind alley." This may turn into the third message, the put-down, if it is framed as an attack on another student. Put-downs, of course, need to be called immediately: "You can't say things like that here. We're not going to build ourselves up by putting others down."

However, the first of those three messages is not a bad one. The student likes to use his brain and be clever. We're not opposed to that. The problem comes from the second message, the derailing of the conversation. Our goal must be to harness that cleverness and redirect it to the service of the subject.

When I listen to students' classroom one-liners, I'm amazed by how often they *unconsciously* reveal a worthwhile take on the topic. After all, a joke requires a bit of critical distance and a perception of irony or incongruity. Those aren't bad kinds of thinking. In fact, we would very much like to encourage those thoughts, but the student who doesn't see himself as a true English student isn't likely to realize the value of the thought he has just had, so it becomes a joke. When we hear that happening, we have to grab the idea and show the student how valuable his thinking really is. This is the strategy I suggested for the Fruitopia joke in the previous chapter.

Another example occurred in my own classroom, as we were studying *Macbeth*. One day I asked, "What do you think about the role Lady Macbeth is playing so far?"

From the side of the room, Danny muttered, "What a witch!" The students around him tittered.

At that point, I could have said, "Danny, if you have something to say, put up your hand." He probably wouldn't have, and that would have been the end of it.

Instead, I pounced.

"Did the rest of you hear that? Danny, can you say that louder?"

Danny tried to wave me off. "Sorry. It was nothing. Just a joke."

"Oh, I know you thought it was a joke, but the back of your mind may be telling you something useful." To the rest of the class, I said, "Danny said she was a witch. Now, we already have three witches in this play. Let's take Danny's joke seriously, and see what happens if we think of Lady Macbeth as the fourth witch. Danny, I wonder why your mind made that connection?"

And, of course, Danny's off-the-cuff remark opened up a valuable way of understanding this character. Not every offhand remark turns out to be so useful, but it happens often enough to repay our attention. We have to listen hard to students who haven't learned to trust their ability to join in the talk of the English classroom. We can teach them that they don't have to laugh off their own thoughts, that they can plug their thinking into the classroom instead of directing it away from the subject.

Emotion Talk

As we saw in Chapter 2, most boys don't get as many chances as girls to practice emotion talk. From an early age, parents are more likely to discuss feelings with female children. Then children begin sorting themselves out into same-sex play groups—boys are especially careful about defining this boundary (Maccoby 1998, 24–30)—which means they're spending most of their time with kids who talk the same way they do, and a gulf appears between the two sexes. Many girls become able to talk about subtle feelings while boys become tongue-tied. This makes it harder to write a character study for English class, and if you believe that being able to name something gives it reality, then the lack of vocabulary for emotions has serious consequences for boys' understanding of themselves and their relationships.

In *The Men They Will Become*, Eli Newberger writes:

> *When a vocabulary of feelings in young boys is missing in their upbringing, they risk growing up to become men at the mercy of their impulses. They remain unaware of their feelings and inarticulate about them. Until we can apply commonly understood words to things, we can't be fully conscious of them. Every step to a higher level of awareness in relationships requires more sophisticated command of language. (1999, 66)*

Dan Kindlon and Michael Thompson speak of their counseling practices, in which they every day meet with boys who are "unversed in the subtleties of emotional language and expression and threatened by emotional complexity" (1999, 3). Daniel Goleman describes a condition known as alexithymia, in which the patient has feelings but cannot put them into words. The lack of words makes emotions "baffling and overwhelming, something to avoid at all costs" (1995, 51). This is a neurological disorder, but such sicknesses often tell us something about the functions of healthy brains. If there is a circuit that allows us to make the connection of words with feelings, even "normal" people may have stronger or weaker versions of the circuitry. Many of us know what it's like to draw a blank when asked to identify our feelings, and we may sympathize with "the alexithymic's dilemma: having no words for feelings means not making the feelings your own" (52).

There come times when we need to give a student a little bit of language—just a few words—and that gift opens up room for thought. Here is a story about a student who needed to be shown how to talk.

My grade 11 students had just finished their job-shadowing assignment, each spending a day with an adult at a work location. Their task was then to deliver a ten-minute oral report, telling the class what they found out about the career. Charles had spent his day with a cardiologist. When it came time to talk about possible drawbacks of the job, Charles became uncomfortable.

"You're dealing with people who have heart disease. So you might get to know them. And then they die. So you might . . . like . . . cry or something? I don't know," he trailed off sheepishly. There was gentle, understanding laughter from some of his classmates, appreciating the awkwardness of this moment for Charles, and he hurried on, with relief, to his next point. (What was the problem? What didn't he "know"? Was he moving into areas of experience that were beyond his understanding? Or was it a shortage of language—a recognition that "crying or something" didn't quite get at what he was trying to say?)

At the end of his report, I said, "I want to come back to the question of his emotional involvement. After all, a cardiologist *is* going to see people who are going to die. That must be difficult. Painful, maybe." I was planting words for his use, to see if he could push his thought any further.

Charles straightened in his seat and said, "Yes, it *is* a difficulty. He has to care about his patients and want them to do well. He feels involved, and to see someone die because you couldn't do more to help them must hurt. But it is part of the job for him and he has to learn how to handle that difficulty." What a different way to talk! He had used a few of my words as a springboard to pull together his own thoughts more articulately. Before, Charles had been eager to move on, and the class had delicately let the subject drop, but now that Charles had some control over what he was saying, hands went up and his classmates wanted to pursue the issue. At first, Charles had seemed embarrassed to have stumbled into an area of emotional life that he couldn't handle; a teacher's gift of a few words let him have a second, more dignified run at the topic.

(Incidentally, boys in this class generally took the position that professionals have to separate the person from the disease; girls mostly argued that such separation wouldn't be healthy and that they wanted a doctor who cared about them as a person. This split typifies a male tendency to compartmentalize versus a female preference to connect; you probably have your own opinion on this debate, but I don't think either bias is wrong.)

Building vocabulary has always been in the English teacher's job description, and once we recognize this lack in many boys' language, we can put particular emphasis on the language of emotions. The need, first of all, is to generate *many* words. Boys often like to solve problems quickly, so when they're asked to describe a character in literature, they're happy to find just one label to slap onto the character. Or two. Or three, if they must. We have to insist on the *richness* of inner experience and devise tasks that demand the generation of lots of words. Here are some possibilities.

- Have students draw a picture of a character on a big piece of paper and then fill it with words describing the character's emotions.

- Teach about icebergs being seven-eighths under the water: what we see of a person is only the tip of the iceberg. What are the words for that other seven-eighths? Actually draw the iceberg on the blackboard and have them draw it in their notebooks.

- Try geological analogies. Earth is composed of layers. Can we represent a character by layers of experience or feeling? Are some layers deeper than others? Is there a core? In geology, when layers rub up against each other, you can get an earthquake. Is that a useful analogy for this character?

- Try the jewel analogy. A jewel has several sides, and you can't see them all at the same time. What are those sides? Which can't be seen simultaneously? (With younger students, you might want to have an oversized mock-up of a multifaceted jewel for them to label.)

- Watch just a few minutes of a film at the point where a major revelation or reversal occurs. (Courtroom scenes work well.) Get students to name *all* the emotions that flicker across characters' faces. (Use the pause button to catch all the fleeting expressions.)

- Once the words are out there, you can work on sorting or categorizing the words. Which words go together? Which seem contradictory? How can we understand those contradictions?

In the end, we want students to understand that inner experience is rich, complex, and varied and that we can talk about that. Part of the blockage for boys is the feeling that they don't know what to say, and putting vocabulary into their hands is the first step toward making them feel more confident about that kind of talk.

However, just having lots of words and spending lots of time talking about feelings and inner qualities doesn't guarantee that boys will *want* to have these discussions. There are still powerful cultural forces telling them, on one side, that real men don't talk about this stuff, and, on the other side, that they're going to look like fools in the eyes of girls if they speak clumsily about feelings. Even when they have plenty of vocabulary, there's still a good chance of boys being frozen on the spot if asked for a feeling response. As a male colleague told me, "When someone asks me what I'm feeling, I think, 'Let me out of here.'"

That brings us to the golden rules for dealing with boys and feelings: the "double Ds"—*delay* and *deflect*.

The First D: Delay

The story about Charles' report on the cardiologist wasn't just about language. If you look back at that anecdote, you'll notice that timing was an issue as well. I didn't push Charles at the moment of his embarrassment; instead, I let him finish his prepared report and only then brought him back to the question of a doctor's feelings.

Men do have feelings, and they can talk about them, but there may be a delay before that can happen. This phenomenon has been widely noted by popular writers on gender communication. Deborah Tannen, for example, gives examples of husbands who initially tell their wives there's nothing to speak of, but later reveal important emotional information: "For men, 'Nothing' may be a ritual response at the start of a conversation" (1990, 80). In *A Fine Young Man*, Michael Gurian says that the urge for immediate action forces a delay in the processing of feelings:

> It is often a delayed-reaction emotionality and thus is a source of difficulty when males and females try to relate to each other. Females tend to process the emotional content of a situation—an argument, a moving film, a social interchange—long before the male does. (1998, 35)

In *Real Boys*, William Pollack says that if we want to get behind the mask of the Boys Code, we have to accept the boy's own "emotional schedule" (1998, 8). Particularly when feelings are difficult, confused, or painful, there is likely to be what he calls a "timed-silence syndrome," and a parent or teacher who tries to intrude too soon will succeed only in locking up the boy's ability to express himself (102).

Of course, we're not talking about *all* emotions being delayed. Announce that there's a surprise school holiday tomorrow, and boys will have no difficulty figuring out how to cheer immediately, and males are especially prone to flaming into sudden anger or violence when they are insulted. But those are predictable, straightforward responses. In English classes we ask them to think about emotional situations that are subtler, more complex, ambiguous, even contradictory. That's when they need time.

I don't think we have to see this delay as a male deficit or disability. It's not an absolute negative. It's a drawback only when they're in situations that value on-the-spot emoting. If you were having emergency surgery, you'd probably prefer the surgeon to put his or her feelings on hold and just do the job. It might be that some English classrooms idealize emotional display, but I don't think it *has* to be that way. We don't want to encourage snap, superficial, judgmental responses, which may be the best we can hope for if we insist on instant emotion. We don't want to slip in to a caricature of the sensitive English teacher: "Now that we've just read that poem, how does it make you feel? Come on, emote for me!" Surely, there are other ways of timing responses.

Do you remember the scene in *Macbeth* (Act II, scene iii) when the murder of Duncan has been discovered? Macbeth, the murderer, declares how his feelings are stirred by this horrible event, and just about everyone is running around emoting, talking about how terrible he or she feels. Everyone, that is, except the ones most deeply touched—Duncan's sons, Malcolm and Donalbain. Malcolm seems confused by his own silence, and quietly asks his brother why the two of them have nothing to say. Donalbain has a shrewder understanding of psychology. He recognizes the possibility of treachery in all this talk about feelings; as for themselves, he says, "Our tears are not yet brewed." That's a very male moment, with its instinctive distrust of emotion talk that leaps too easily to the tongue and its recognition of a need for brewing time.

How can English teachers build in safe delays—brewing time—for boys?

1. Work on analysis first, feelings later.

It has been observed that many American teachers use "reader response" techniques, which often include feeling responses, as a way of *beginning* discussion of a piece of literature, as a *lead-in* to more traditional analysis (Applebee 1993, 201). "Let's have a gut response," we begin, perhaps as a motivational device, before moving on to the "thinking" stuff. From the point of view of male psychology, *that may be exactly the wrong sequence.* Sometimes we can start with feelings, because some works do have a strong immediate impact, and certainly there are some students for whom the emotional response is the first hook. But sometimes we should reverse the sequence and give a break to those students who need to start with something more concrete or more analytic. A British study of fourteen schools that have developed effective methods for teaching English to boys identified "beginning with analytical tasks, *before* discussing feelings or empathy" as a key feature of their practice (Frater 1998, 73).

Here's one example. Sometimes we read a passage and say, "Now what's the mood (or tone) of that paragraph (or poem)?" *Mood* and *tone* are slippery, emotional concepts. Some students get it almost instinctively; others don't. It's possible to delay that question by first doing a little sorting and classification. "Let's just make a list of all the nouns, verbs, adjectives, and adverbs in that paragraph, and when that's done we'll see if they fit into any patterns." By the time students see a list of words with particular sets of connotations, they might be more ready to recognize the mood.

Here's another example. Sometimes we ask students how they feel about a certain character right after they read a story. (And often girls' hands go up to answer the question.) Then we go on to unpack the reasons for that response. We could do it in the reverse order. We could start instead by saying, "Let's list all the decisions the main character made, why he made those decisions, and what were the consequences of each decision." That's a manageable analytic framework, and *after* that's done, everyone might be in a better position to consider carefully how he or she feels about the character.

Many of us who go into English teaching may be the kinds of readers who are quick with instinctive responses. Sometimes we need to back off from those instincts and think more analytically about what might be the components of text (or life) that lead to responses and help students work through those components in order to brew their own feelings.

How long should the delay be? It varies. Maybe five minutes is enough, if enough thinking has happened in those five minutes to allow feelings to percolate. Maybe it needs to be several hours: do the analysis in class, then ask students to formulate a thoughtful response as homework. (Homework has the advantage of allowing time and privacy for the generation of a response. It has the disadvantage that boys are generally less conscientious than girls about doing homework [Head 1999, 69; Evans 1996].) Sometimes the most fruitful delay will be weeks or months, as we see in the next section.

2. Construct a curriculum that allows feelings to build over time.
Too often our courses consist of one little unit after another, a fragmented mosaic that doesn't necessarily add up to a big picture. In *Curriculum as*

Conversation, Arthur Applebee envisions a program in which conversations begin to "echo back on one another" over time, where there is enough continuity for students to find themselves in November reassessing what they read and thought in September (1996, 77). There is much to be said for such a curriculum. For one thing, students would be constructing a larger cognitive structure, which leads to greater depth of learning. From the point of view of feelings, it allows for related experiences—reading, writing, discussion, thinking—to accumulate over time, so that whatever emotional response there is will be deepened, enriched, and truly educated, rather than being the flashy, quick responses that some students do well and some can't pull off at all.

A few years ago, I taught in a school where the grade 12 general (that is, nonacademic) course was structured around the theme of Turning Points. We talked about lots of other things as well, but we always came back to the idea of people going through significant changes in their lives. The theme had obvious relevance for young people at the end of their high school careers. Their largest project for the year was to write a sizable reflective paper about a turning point that had been important to them in their lives so far. I told them it didn't have to be *the most* important turning point, because I wasn't trying to force them to talk about things that were none of my business. All they had to do was choose *an* important moment, one that they would be comfortable writing about for my eyes only.

I always briefly announced this project at the very beginning of the year, in September, but it wasn't due, and they wouldn't start working on it, until months later, in April or May. In the meantime, we went on with the course material, talking about turning points experienced by people like Tom Wingfield in *The Glass Menagerie* or the Lomans in *Death of a Salesman*. The final projects that came in from these students were invariably the best-written, most polished work they had done all year—probably the best work many of them had ever done in high school. What I recall most is the emotional drain on me as I read my way through paper after paper that was moving, delicate, and frank in the expression of feeling. Remember, these were general-level students, heading off not to university, but to the workplace or apprenticeships. There were lots of "tough" guys—cigarette packs in their pockets, drinking and fighting on the weekends—and these boys would devastate me with how powerfully and precisely they could command the language of feeling.

It was years ago and I didn't keep any of those papers, so I can't really quote them, but I remember young Brad, who always seemed suspicious and cynical. Brad wrote about his father, who used to promise to take him fishing and camping and "all that other father and son stuff they do on TV." Brad's turning point was the tender and bitter realization that those things weren't ever going to happen. And I remember Jim's paper. Jim went into a coffee shop one evening and discovered his father with some woman that Jim didn't know. That was the beginning of the end of his family.

I can't imagine getting better writing from these students: it was "literate" in the usual English teacher sense, but it was also emotionally literate. My point is that this work happened at the *end* of the course, after they had had about eight months to talk about and analyze fictional stories, eight months for the idea to sit and brew in the back of their minds.

I'm sure this assignment wouldn't have worked at the beginning of the course. There is trust that needs to be built up between teacher and student, but there's also time needed for thinking and feeling. I know there's one school of thought that says, "Start with the personal and then move to the literature." If I were following that line of thinking, I might have *started* the course by asking them all to write a little piece about a turning point in their own lives, but the writing would have been superficial and guarded, and I knew I wouldn't want to come in cold and have to write such a thing about myself. Instead, we started in September *impersonally*, brainstorming a list of all the kinds of turning points people—people in general—go through. Then we turned to the literature. Then, finally, much later, we turned to ourselves. And then they were ready.

The Second D: Deflect

British studies of successful English and language arts programs for boys consistently emphasize the importance of building "well-conceived elements of drama into the teaching" (Frater 1998, 74; see also Arnot et al. 1998, 29; Penny 1998, 87; QCA 1998, 33).

One reason for including drama is the fact that boys like to be engaged physically. Sports offer physical activity, and video games often involve the body in some way: you're in the driver's seat and you have the controls or the weapons in your hands. Among computer games, boys prefer combat and sports simulation games by a wide margin; girls show little interest in this kind of entertainment (Millard 1997, 72). For some boys, it is only when they are physically engaged that they feel they're actually *doing* something, as was found in one study of bright but underachieving boys: they didn't dislike learning *per se* but were turned off by teaching styles that didn't get them up and "doing something" (Bleach 1998a, 39).

That's reason enough to consider including drama in the English classroom, but we need to be careful about letting the need for physical activity be the *only* rationale for drama. Sometimes that kind of thinking condescends to boys, as if they're wild animals and just need to knock around a bit to let off steam. If that's all they need, then just acting out a scene from a story is good enough, especially if there's a chase or a swordfight: it wouldn't matter whether they were actually *learning* anything, wouldn't matter whether they understood the story any better after the exercise. Indeed, too much classroom drama is probably of this act-out-a-scene-from-the-book variety. Students certainly have fun, but we might be hard-pressed to prove that they understand the literature any better. (I have discussed the uses and misuses of classroom drama elsewhere; see Pirie 1997.) At its most reduced form, the need to let boys be physical leads to advice that boys should be given chances to hand deliver messages to the office or clean the chalkboards—any chance to use their bodies. It's not that these are bad things to do, but they're only about containment; they're not really about educating.

Well-designed drama is more than an opportunity for boys to stretch their limbs. Good drama activities invite students to step into role and combine what they know (from their own lives in the "real" world) with the new or fictional framework offered by the drama. For students who are uncomfortable talking about their *own* feelings, drama offers rich opportunities to be someone else or somewhere else, and to *deflect* the expression of feelings into a fictitious form. This is the second D, the second golden rule for dealing with emotions: if feelings can be *deflected* through role-playing, unexpected fluency may result.

Here is a story from a grade 10 classroom. We were studying Shakespeare's *Twelfth Night* and were just a few scenes into the play. I asked students to brainstorm questions they might like to ask Viola if we could make that character come alive and talk to us. After a list of questions had been generated, I asked if we could have a volunteer play the role of Viola and try to improvise answers, right on the spot, while the class asked those questions. I promised that if the role-player had difficulties, he or she could ask for a time-out and we would help come up with the answers.

Chris, a boy, volunteered. Chris was a typical fifteen-year-old: chunky football player, didn't say much in English class, liked to read car magazines. He may have volunteered as a joke, and the class hooted good-naturedly as he came forward to the hot seat.

Students began asking their questions and Chris answered in role as Viola. He was doing fairly well, and then someone said, "You know, we haven't seen anything very attractive about this Duke Orsino, but you have fallen in love with him. Could you, Viola, please explain to us what you find so attractive about the Duke?"

The class collectively smirked, anticipating the spectacle of our Chris explaining why he found a man attractive.

Chris thought for only a second, then launched into a beautiful ode to the mystery of love: how it comes like a sudden shaft of sunlight and cannot be bound by logical explanations or common reason, how they would never understand it until they too had their worlds illuminated and saw with new eyes.

It was all spontaneous and it was stunningly beautiful. The class applauded in genuine appreciation. And it was very good understanding of Shakespearean comedy, because love does come out of nowhere in those plays. What fine understanding, what eloquent expression—from a boy. A boy playing a role. If we had been just talking, out of role, in regular class discussion, I'm sure he never would have expressed that understanding. From his own mouth, it would have seemed too soft, too sensitive, too feminine. In fact, I don't even know whether he would have recognized that understanding in himself, even silently. It took the role-playing to unlock him, allowing him to deflect his understanding through the role.

I've seen similar scenes—the silent becoming eloquent in role, the awkward becoming gracious—often enough that I've come to wonder whether there's any such thing as the truly inarticulate person, or whether it's only that we're always playing roles and some roles allow us to be articulate and some roles don't. Men who are confident speakers on a podium suddenly seem inept at small talk. Women who chat easily with their friends freeze at the thought of speaking publicly (Tannen 1990, 86–88). I once had a student who stuttered painfully in class and in social situations, but he was one of the school's best actors; on stage, his stutter disappeared. He told me, "It's as if it's not me speaking; it's the role."

Teenagers are notoriously trying out roles for themselves, and some masculine roles have strictly policed rules about what you can and cannot say. We shouldn't make the mistake of thinking that that means boys can't *ever* say or think those thoughts.

When the actor Michael J. Fox left the television series *Spin City*, there was a special farewell episode. In real life, the actor was leaving to join the fight against Parkinson's disease, from which he suffers. This was widely publicized, and everyone watching the show knew that there was an extra level of emotion: as the character Mike Flaherty struggles with the ordeal of saying good-bye to the other characters, we know that this is also the real Michael J. Fox saying good-bye to his colleagues. The episode focuses on the expression and suppression of emotions. Near the end of the episode, characters sit at a table in a bar, struggling with their feelings. ("I just don't think we need to get all misty about it," says one.)

Mike's boss, the mayor, isn't there at the bar, but finally Mike goes to the mayor's office and finds that a videocamera is set up in the room.

The mayor explains, "You know how uncomfortable I am expressing my feelings, so I thought I'd say good-bye to you on video." Even though Mike is now there in the flesh, the mayor still turns to the videocamera and delivers a moving farewell—"I could never say this to your face. . . ." His words are possible only because he directs them to the camera, not to the real Michael, sitting there beside him. Finally, the mayor ends his speech, stops the machine, pulls out the tape, and hands it to Michael, saying brusquely, "There you go." He's back in his taciturn masculine mode.

This scene was, I thought, an insightful, comic portrayal of masculine emotion. The feelings are genuine but can surface only when deflected through the camera. Yes, ultimately, it would be better if the words could be spoken directly, without deflection, but in the meantime I'm happy to unlock students any way I can, only too glad to surprise them into eloquence.

Of course, role-playing can happen on paper as well: students can write in role, without any physical involvement at all, although that probably doesn't have quite the power of really playing the role. In my example of Chris playing Viola, you'll notice that this wasn't a physically taxing role for Chris. All he had to do was sit in a chair and answer some questions, but he was involved in the sense that he became the embodiment of a character. I think we have to be careful about the physical activity angle of classroom drama: it's not that boys need a sweaty workout in English class, but they do need a chance to feel that they are engaged in the lesson. Some of the most important action that we're interested in is, in fact, *inner* action—struggles of emotion, conscience, and will—and this inner action can be dramatized through small gestures of external action.

To take a commonly taught novel, the boys in *Lord of the Flies* find themselves torn between conflicting emotions, even conflicting versions of themselves. Those versions can be embodied in the classroom, physicalizing the subtleties of the inner drama. I ask students to choose groups of three and find a space to stand in the room. I remind them that people have different feelings at different times and ask them to work together with their partners to shape one member of the group into a statue or sculpture that represents one version of Ralph on the island, one side of him that we know about from reading the novel. (I point out that a statue of Ralph blowing the conch is too obvious and should be avoided.) Since this is a living sculpture, they are then asked to add a small element of meaningful movement, perhaps just a turn of the head or a shrug of the shoulders. This movement can be repeated constantly, like a few seconds of videotape being looped through endless replay.

After that living statue has been perfected, I ask each group to choose now some *other* aspect of Ralph, some different side of his personality or other set of feelings, and to repeat the previous steps, this time shaping a second group member into a statue of that new aspect. I suggest that they look for a second aspect that is in some way an interesting pairing or contrast to their first statue.

Once groups have polished their living statues, we give each group a chance to show us what they have prepared. The two statues take their positions and perform their movements, while the third member of the team explains to the class what the group intended to show through its representations. Typical pairings might include the early Ralph in effortless control of the mob versus Ralph fighting for control at the end of the book, or responsible Ralph hard at work making huts versus Ralph being swept up momentarily by the bloody excitement of the hunt. Not every pair will be profound, but by the end you will have a room full of different images that, taken together, embody the rich range of Ralph's inner life. Of course, you can repeat the exercise with Jack or other major characters from the novel.

Once again, this is a physical activity, but there's actually very little movement. I like working with statues and tableaux, sometimes with tiny minimalist movements, because this *slows down* the overt action of a story and allows us to pay closer attention to subtleties. I have little interest in letting kids act out the scenes of gross action offered by the novel. The chases and pig stabbings and the violent "dance" that ends Simon's life are all tempting bits of action, but kids performing those scenes are likely to be caught up in the spectacle and produce only amateurish mockeries. We can't try to compete with film and television in supplying violent spectacle for kids. If we try to play that game, we'll lose, because the visual media will always do it better than we can in the classroom, even if we choose action novels to read. The special thing that we have to offer is reflection on the inner life of individuals and the relationships of people in communities, and we can use dramatization to make that understanding more accessible to all our students.

I especially value this *Lord of the Flies* statue activity, which can be applied to just about any narrative, because it manifests the array of complex and contradictory things that can be going on inside a character. A lot of the difficulty with gender roles in our society comes from our habit of trying to oversimplify feelings and roles: "Boys are X, not Y. Girls are Y, not X. Boys feel A, but never B." An exercise like the one I have described lays bare the reality that our identities are multifaceted and shifting and that the life of the emotions is varied and sometimes puzzling. That, of course, is a lesson not just about literature but about the emotional lives of our students themselves, deflected, refracted through literature and dramatic technique.

5 *Voodoo and Gibber-Jabber*

Writing

Several years ago, I was conducting a class readaround in a senior writing course, with all of us sharing pieces we had just written. One girl read out a fine, sizzlingly passionate poem, and when she finished there was an immediate response from an exceptionally expressive young man named Oliver.

"That's amazing!" exclaimed Oliver. "That's so good! But I don't how you do it. I'd give anything to be able to write like that, but I just don't know how it's done." (You see why I say he was exceptionally expressive: many boys would not be so frank about publicly admitting that they didn't know how to do something.)

The student couldn't tell Oliver how she did it, but that day something clicked for me. Of course he didn't know how it was done: he'd never *seen* anyone write a poem. Sure, he'd studied poems in school after they'd been constructed, but simply looking at a painting by Rembrandt doesn't tell you how to make one yourself. He'd even been in the same room as people who were writing poems, but it was all happening silently inside their heads. There was no way he could know how anyone did this mysterious thing.

The next day, I came in and said, "I'm going to show you what happens when I write a poem. It's different for different people, but at least you'll see one person's process." I picked a topic (I forget what it was—something ready at hand like a picture on the wall or the weather outside) and started writing on the blackboard, talking my thoughts aloud all the while. Students watched me struggling with structure and word choice, discovering, with their help, what I wanted to say. By the end of class, there was a poem on the blackboard. Believe me, it wasn't a very good poem, but it clearly was a poem, and they had seen it being made. It wasn't a mysterious creation handed down from the Muses on Olympus. It was an object constructed by human hands, and they knew what went in to its making. Best of all, afterward, they said with some surprise, "Well, *I* could do *that*!"

I realized there was something here that they hadn't heard before: the real story of how a poem might be made. I began to wonder how often we have glossed over the inner workings of literacy, *telling* students to generate, create, organize, develop, elaborate, expand, explain, conclude, or whatever, without always *showing* students *how* those things are done.

To repeat, I don't mean simply holding up finished examples of good writing. It's certainly worthwhile to see exemplars of good organization, elaboration, inventiveness, and so on, but that by itself amounts to no more than holding up a Rembrandt and saying, "Now let's see you do that." We also need to be clear about the steps one takes to achieve such excellence. Indeed, it may seem to us, at exasperated moments, that we have to be *painfully* clear, but that's only because we're already good at the subject and can take those steps for granted. In fact, you and I were probably the students who were already good at reading and writing and never did need to unpack the processes for ourselves. The things we did as English students just came naturally, as they do for some, but not all, of our students.

Voodoo Pedagogy

If we leave those processes of reading and writing cloaked in mystery, telling ourselves that it all either comes naturally or else it doesn't, we surrender to voodoo pedagogy. In voodoo, privileged people, objects, and rituals are invested with secret magical power, and to some of our students it certainly seems that there must be mysterious, unnamed powers needed to do well in English.

One teacher reported the following conversation with a student she was trying to help. She said to the student, "You know, the stuff you need to do for your English teacher isn't magic."

The boy shot back, "Yes, it *is* magic, Miss. Some kids always get As. I always get Cs and I never know why. It *is* magic."

A consistent theme in the research on boys' learning is the need for *explicit* instruction: clearly defined, step-by-step guidelines (Bleach 1998b, 45; Frater 1998, 73; QCA 1998, 33). To let students in on the secret of what happens when we read and write, we must take processes that are often left unspoken and make them explicit. Doing that gives power to the person who learns the secret—the power to do things with texts. Boys like to have power. They like to learn the secret of how things work, and they like things to be explicit.

For many boys, this is what intimidates them about English: there seems to be a secret code shared between authors, teachers, and some students, especially the girls. These insiders all understand the code and can produce and interpret things with "deep," "sensitive," or "hidden" meanings that leave the boys outside, feeling stupid. Boys don't like to feel stupid—who would?—but they sometimes do, especially around girls, women, and English teachers. Women, it seems to them, often leave things unspoken, expecting men to read between the lines and make intuitive leaps. This makes boys nervous. It's a lot safer in the math classroom, where teachers have a long history of helping students see what steps you have to follow. Math teachers let you in on secrets.

In the rest of this chapter, we'll look at ways we can lay bare some of the secrets of writing—essay writing, poetry writing, story writing—secrets that may be particularly obscure to boys. In later chapters, we'll work at demystifying the voodoo of reading, speaking, and listening. Throughout it all, the underlying issue is how we *think*.

Think-Alouds

The lesson described at the beginning of this chapter, in which I talked my way through the writing of a poem, is sometimes called a think-aloud and can be used for any work where there is a need to make visible what goes on inside people's heads. (See Wilhelm, Baker, and Dube 2001 for another discussion of think-alouds.)

The first step might be a teacher demonstration, as in my example earlier. It's important that the exercise be an authentic one for the teacher: you have to be genuinely struggling with a new writing task. You may have old pieces of your own writing, marked up with editing, stored in your filing cabinet, and while it's good for students to see those drafts, looking at already-drafted pages is not the same as being present at the moment of thinking and writing, witnessing the process moment-by-moment.

Students should see the writer (you) having problems and see how those problems can be handled with patience and a willingness to try out something cautiously but then revise or discard it if it doesn't work. When we're in the midst of the writing process, everything is tentative; nothing is engraved in stone.

Tentativeness is not a macho mind-set. Many men like to feel that they can quickly spot the "right" thing to do. In many situations, this is a good quality: if you work on the floor of the stock market or in emergency services, you'd better be pretty good at making snap decisions and taking quick action. Women, in contrast, are often seen as being more tentative in their speech and action. This has been cast as a negative trait for women seeking acceptance in traditional male settings, resulting in assertiveness training to correct the "problem" (Johnson 1997, 12). However, when we pose "boys in English" as the "problem," a little healthy tentativeness doesn't look so bad after all.

The typically male push for the decisive, quick fix can be a problem when we confront challenges that don't have clear paths to a single right answer, like many writing tasks. The irritation of this uncertainty may cause a boy to freeze up, feeling that he never knows what to say, or he may slap something down onto the page quickly, just to get it over with, and then never return to revise it. He needs "tentativeness training."

This is where a teacher demonstrating a think-aloud can model more useful attitudes. The teacher might say, "Well, I don't really know where to start, but I'm not going to sit here staring at a blank page (or chalkboard), because I know that won't help. So I'm going to put something down, even if it's not brilliant. I know I can come back and change it later." There might be little detours: "That reminds me of something that I can't really use yet, but I'll just jot it down here at the side so I don't forget it." Imperfection can be taken in stride: "Yuck! That sounds terrible, doesn't it? Well, leave it for now. I'm glad no one has to see it except you guys."

By the end of the lesson, the chalkboard or the overhead transparency should be a mess, full of cross-outs and arrows, before the piece can be transcribed neatly. For boys who get frozen by not knowing what to do right away, it can be a revelation to see a teacher going ahead, making a mess and tolerating it, even embracing it, and happily returning later to make improvements.

After an initial teacher demonstration, responsibility for thinking aloud must be passed on to the students themselves, so that they may practice and internalize this writerly talk. Students can work in pairs to create short pieces of writing together, talking their way through the process. Too often, we have a romantic view of the writer, barricaded away in a lonely attic, but this vision of the solitary writer has almost no educational use. Learning is a social activity, heavily dependent on working with others who can maybe do something a bit better than we can ourselves. (See Vygotsky 1978.)

For shared writing activities to work well, students probably shouldn't choose their own writing partners, which too often results in boys working with boys, and weak students working with other weak students. We also want to avoid the danger of the better writer dominating the work, while the weaker student gets a free ride. I address this problem openly, telling students that the value of the exercise lies in the talk that goes on between the coauthors: "If your partner says, 'Let's just put this here because it's better that way,' and you don't understand *why* it's better, then it's your job to stop him and make him share his thinking. *Challenge* him, if you have to." Both partners benefit: the weaker students see how better writers work, and, we hope, begin to share in that work, while the better writers are forced to make their processes explicit even to themselves. This metacognition—thinking about their own thinking—is worthwhile learning for all students.

Explicit? Yes. Simplistic? No.

When I talk to teachers about making the writing process explicit, looking for the step-by-step pathways, teachers sometimes leap in and say, "Oh, yes! I have a great little gimmick for getting students to write poetry. They fill in the blanks on my handout and in just five minutes they have a poem." Or, "I have a wonderful formula for essay writing. I call it 'Six Easy Steps to the Five-Paragraph Essay.'"

That's when I get worried. When I speak of being explicit about what's involved in writing, I mean *honestly* showing students what *actually* goes on when people write. In our effort to help boys see the steps by which writing occurs, we must resist the temptation to replace authentic practices with gamelike replicas of real writing. I'm not trying to make writing easy or simple, if that means providing formulaic gimmicks that disguise the real difficulties of writing. It *isn't* easy to write a poem or an essay, and I don't think boys need to be tricked into believing that it is easy. Boys don't have to be afraid of challenges, as long as they can see what needs to be done.

When we provide those simplistic gimmicks, we mean well. We don't want to see our students stumped, so we try to smooth the path for them. Structuring an essay is hard work, so we suggest a five-paragraph formula, with three body paragraphs. We never meant to suggest that all essays should have three and only three main points, but we forget that early teaching has lasting impact. When students are first learning and struggling with a new practice, they take firm hold of anything that looks like help. Misconceptions introduced at the time of first teaching are appallingly persistent and hard to pry loose in later years.

Mark, a bright senior student, wrote a paper about the factors influencing his reading of a particular work. He declared in his introduction that "three main factors" contributed to his reading: "These factors are my life experiences, the lifestyle that I have been brought up in, and generally the type of person that I am." I pointed out that these categories blended "mushily" together and seemed to be three ways of saying the same thing. When Mark rewrote his paper, he rethought his structure from scratch and, in the cover letter attached to the revision, identified the problem.

I agree with what you said about the mush and I was sort of thinking the same thing when I wrote that line. I had that line because I wanted to have a thesis that would allow for three main points. (I know, it sounds stupid.) I guess that is sort of a reflection on how I sometimes try to fol-low the "rules" of essay writing too strictly.

I'm concerned by the number of senior students, especially boys, who still believe that all essays have to have three body paragraphs. It's as if they've got hold of a ritual—a voodoo ritual—and are afraid to give it up. Since many boys find writing difficult, their need for quick fixes makes them grasp tenaciously, desperately, onto the apparent lifeboat of the five-paragraph formula. Boys like highly structured, rule-governed activities (Gilbert and Gilbert 1998, 80), but that means we have to be careful: anything we offer that looks like a rule had better be *right*—an authentic description of how writing happens—not just a temporary lifesaver. We see a similar warning in a research review of gender differences.

> *Boys show greater adaptability to more traditional approaches to learn-ing which require memorizing abstract, unambiguous facts and rules that have to be acquired quickly. They also appear to be more willing to sac-rifice deep understanding, which requires sustained effort, for correct answers achieved at speed. (Arnot et al. 1998, 28)*

In other words, if we offer boys a quick shortcut that bypasses deeper understanding of writing, they may remember only the shortcut and never find their way to the deeper understanding.

How, then, can we teach essay writing in a way that honestly lays the process out on the table, addressing boys' need for explicit steps with-out falling into the temptation of providing simplistic rules or spurious rituals? To answer that, we first have to look more closely at the way some boys think.

Two Ways of Thinking

The appetite for rules is tied up with a male fondness for abstract logic, a characteristic that has a growth spurt in the adolescent years (Newberger 1999, 207). Many observers have noted that there is a male thinking style that includes a tendency to argue from abstract principles rather than from the messiness of real examples (Tannen 1990, 92), a taste for deductive rather than inductive thinking (Gurian 1998, 181–82), a preference for the supposedly clean answers of math and science, and the celebration of distanced objectivity and disinterested reason (Belenky et al. 1997, 109–10).

There is no doubt that these kinds of thinking are valuable, but they're not the only patterns of thought possible and they're not always helpful when applied to the work of the English class. In particular, the eagerness to jump to generalized conclusions as quickly as possible may short-circuit the thinking we would like to see, preventing boys from patiently working through the richness and complexity of the material being studied (Bowman 1992, 81). They leap for the generalization, then find themselves at a loss, wondering what else they're supposed to say.

This is illustrated by two grade 11 examination answers, one from a boy and one from a girl. The question read:

> *In* Romeo and Juliet, *Shakespeare examines the difficulties young people have when dealing with adult authority figures. Show to what extent you agree or disagree with this statement. Support your ideas with clear, concrete references from the play.*

This question has already offered a generalization about the play—that it is about the difficulties of youth facing adult authority. In the following excerpts from a boy's answer, Derek agrees with the generalization but doesn't know what to do after he has expressed his agreement. His answer begins:

> *Starting with Romeo and Juliet's love for one another one can easily see that their love is ruled by adult authority. The simple reason that their love is forbidden because of their parents would suggest that. It is because of Romeo and Juliet's parents that they must have such a secret relationship instead of an open one. This action easily shows that if this relationship was revealed to their parents consequences would no doubt immediately follow. This shows that they, Romeo and Juliet, have a difficulty of dealing with adult authority, which in this case is their parents.*

Of course, examination conditions don't allow time for real revision and we have to forgive some redundancy, but we sense that Derek is already spinning his wheels. He has been given his generalization and it sounds right to him: it's all "easily" seen and "simple," and he doesn't know what he's supposed to do now.

He struggles on through his answer, mentioning briefly the obvious examples of conflict between the generations. He sees this conflict as a necessary consequence of the older generation's duty to harness youth. As a principle, this makes sense, and it's not a bad way of thinking about the role of elders in Shakespearean drama, but Derek can't reach below the level of the general principle, to the "clear, concrete references" demanded by the question. By the end, his use of uppercase letters hints that he's practically yelling in frustration at his implied audience, an audience so obtuse that it seems to demand a recitation of the obvious.

> *As anyone can see, young people do INDEED have trouble dealing with adult authority. This can be seen throughout the arguments I have presented throughout the story of Romeo and Juliet. . . . It would be crazy to deny that conflicts exist between the young and the old.*

In stark contrast is Rebecca's answer to the same question. Rebecca starts not with the big generalization, but with a specific circumstance—Juliet's upbringing—and goes on to consider how it affects her relationship with authority.

> *In her tender years, Juliet was not raised by her birth mother, Lady Capulet. Society at the time did not permit such a thing to occur and therefore a nurse was employed to look after the child. Being deprived of her mother's company and care, Juliet was emotionally far removed from Lady Capulet's world. The two weren't granted the opportunity to develop a close relationship. As a result, Juliet experienced difficulty in expressing herself when her mother was present. This was especially evident when Lady Capulet came to talk to Juliet about Paris and his interest in her. The dialogue that ensued clearly showed that Juliet and Lady Capulet had a formal relationship rather than a loving one. The nature of her feelings for her mother prevented Juliet from truthfully announcing her view on matters. Instead, she politely replied that she would be willing to do anything her mother pleased, much as an obedient child answers to an authority figure.*

Rebecca goes on to explore the breakdown between Juliet and her father, then turns to Romeo and notes that his parents are concerned but have to use Benvolio as an intermediary to find out what is happening with their son. From these particulars, she builds an interesting portrait of two generations estranged from each other.

These are two different styles of answers. Derek is clearly struggling, straining to express understanding that he may have. We would probably all recognize Rebecca's answer as the more fluent, well-developed answer. Derek would be helped if he could learn to put the generalization on hold and work instead from the ground up, thinking first of the particulars in the literature and seeing where they lead, rather than taking a shortcut to the general principle and then awkwardly trying to find the evidence to support it.

Writing Essays from the Ground Up

I see too many students worried about finding a thesis when they are just *starting* to work on an assignment. A senior student working on an independent research project, for example, might have a collection of books on "the Beat Generation" or "the Thirties in America," and will come to me and say, "I don't know what to do. I can't figure out a thesis."

I counter, "Have you read the books yet?"

"No."

"Then how could you have a thesis?"

"I always thought you were supposed to start with a thesis."

"No," I reply. "A thesis is a kind of answer to a question. If you haven't read the books, you don't even have a question yet."

The student looks even more worried. "Then how will I know what I'm looking for?"

"At first, you don't. You have to spend some time reading those books. In a few weeks, we can talk about what interests you in your reading. That's what you're looking for."

Somehow, we have managed to make many students believe that they ought to have an answer before they work through the thinking process. That's a particularly tempting and dangerous belief for boys, because they do like to get answers right away and may be impatient with a process that seems to slow down finding the answer and getting the job done. The remedy, I think, is to be as frank as possible about opening up how the process works. Partly, that means helping them see that patiently examining specifics isn't an annoying slowdown. ("That English teacher keeps asking me for more specifics, when I've already made my point. What a nuisance!") Instead, it is the way we find some of the best answers.

I have begun to walk students through a process that shifts them to a more inductive approach. For some boys, it has led to breakthrough realizations about the relationship of specifics to generalities.

First, here's an overview of the process, as I outline it for students.

1. Look for a genuine question arising out of the material.

2. Collect all the evidence that might have any bearing on the question.

3. Sort the evidence into little piles of related ideas; then sort those piles into bigger and bigger piles of connected ideas. (Some pieces of evidence may be left over. This demands a decision: are the leftovers irrelevant, or do they indicate something that needs further thought?)

4. Decide on a tentative thesis. (It may still be a bit fuzzy.)

5. Begin drafting, using the piles as organization. (As you write, the thesis may shift, the organization may need to be shuffled, and you may have to go back and look for further evidence.)

Here's what it looks like in practice.

As we are reading literature—let's say short stories as an example—we keep a record of moments of uncertainty in our readings. These would be moments when there is something confusing, contradictory, or puzzling either in the initial reading or in the subsequent discussion. I tell students that these are moments to be valued, because this is where we catch a glimpse of the complexity in the work, and it is by examination of complexities that we gain our greatest insights. We compare questions, talk about how we might try to answer them, and trace the implications of possible answers.

Through this initial approach, I mean to lay down as a foundation the idea that questions may be more valuable than answers. This is directly counter to the drive for answers that is so often fed by schools. It also faces head-on the male complaint that English is too mushy, that it doesn't have the hard facts and answers of math and science. Some suggest catering to that bias by including more objective questions in the English classroom, but such a strategy would, I think, fail to recognize the movement of intellectual history in our time. In many fields, we are coming to realize that knowledge is complex, not simple, that possibilities and probabilities are more likely than certainties, and that multiple perspectives supplant the old model of objectivity (Marzano et al. 1988, 126). In other words, my message to students is that *the indeterminacy of many things in English is not a reflection of some embarrassing softness in the subject, but rather the reflection of a very contemporary (postmodern, if you like) understanding of the nature of knowledge,* including knowledge in the sciences themselves. Boys may not like mushy vagueness, but they can be interested in the way the mind works. The things in life and literature that do not make full, immediate sense are not airy-fairy "whatever-you-think-is-right" quagmires: they are tough challenges for sharp minds.

When we're ready to try writing an essay, I often don't give the students topics. Teacher-assigned topics too often imply that there's a teacher-approved answer to be found. They've built up their own lists of questions worth pursuing and they choose their topics from those lists. I warn them that any question that seems to have an answer already tucked away in the back of their minds is too easy. I stress that there is genuine *risk* involved in tackling a question for which you don't already know the answer, and that risk is exactly what makes for real learning. (The idea that we grow through facing risks makes sense to boys.)

It is tempting at this point to formulate a thesis and then to try to find the evidence to support it. Indeed, this move is mandated by teachers who instruct students to come up with a thesis early in the writing process. However, looking for a thesis at this point would only confirm the urge to grab too quickly for a generalization. It's exactly what we don't want them to do.

Instead, I use an analogy with police work. When police are trying to solve a mystery, they collect evidence—lots of evidence, some of which may not be useful in the end but nevertheless has to be collected and sorted. The very worst thing that a detective can do is decide too early in the case who is the likeliest guilty party. If the detective does decide that too early, then he or she will begin to look only for evidence that confirms the initial prejudice; contradictory evidence will be ignored. This is exactly what happens in cases of mistaken arrest, and it's also what happens when we tell students to decide on a thesis and then go looking for evidence to support it. Boys are only too willing to settle on an answer and shut down consideration of other possibilities.

I insist that they begin a process of collecting evidence, jotting down notes about anything in the story that might be relevant to their case. I insist that they can't go any further *until I see that they've collected a pile of raw evidence*. This is a crucial step for all those students whose inclination is to start writing without having patiently worked from the ground up. We talk about ways of collecting data: the evidence will need to be sorted later, so separate points on individual file cards can be useful, or they may wish to use the outlining function of a word processor that will allow them to go back later and shuffle their points.

Organization 1: Multiple Patterns

Organizing the "data" they've collected for their essays can be another stumbling block for boys. Boys like to be given structure, but they don't automatically know how to organize ideas themselves (OFSTED 1998, section 2.6). Too often, we vaguely tell students that they have to organize their work, without actually unpacking for them what that means; thus, organization becomes one of those voodoo rituals that exclude boys: some people, it seems to them, have the magic ability to organize, and others simply don't.

In *Classroom Instruction That Works*, Marzano et al. survey research findings about methods that actually make a difference to student learning. It turns out that research strongly indicates the value of explicit practice in classification exercises (2001, 15). This is where the think-aloud technique is particularly useful. As a demonstration, you might bring in a pile of random objects—a stapler, a book, a shoe, a cereal box, a lightbulb—or a selection of unrelated pictures. Then ask a student to sort the objects into categories, talking out his or her thinking all the while. When one classification is set, the student then creates a different set of categories, and another, and another. The class can join in, finding further sets of similarity and difference: color, size, shape, purpose, associated objects, material, texture, commercial value, and more. For the boy who has never known how it is that things get organized, it can be powerful learning to hear what goes on inside people's heads when they're sorting.

When you're finished with staplers and shoes, the class can move on to something closer to the course material. Characters or events from a story can be listed and the same questions asked: "How many different ways of sorting out these events can we think of?" "What purpose would be served by each specific sorting?"

It is important for students to see that there isn't one right categorization, but many possibilities, depending on the *purposes* of the organizer. (A department store would arrange those objects one way, while someone trying to cram them all into a backpack would sort them differently, paying special attention to shape and breakability.) The automatic instinct of some boys is to look for the one right way, but more powerful and transferable learning—mindful rather than mindless learning—results from entertaining a range of possible answers. (Psychologist Ellen Langer writes about the importance of learners playing with possibilities in *The Power of Mindful Learning* [1997].) Stressing that there are many viable groupings highlights the active role of the sorter—the one who *constructs meaning* according to his or her purposes. This is what is meant by a constructivist approach: an approach that makes learners conscious of their own participation in the act of making meaning.

Organization 2: Visual Patterns

Many boys have particular strength in interpreting visual material such as charts and diagrams (Head 1999, 72). This includes a variety of visual organizers that can be useful in finding shapes for thoughts: comparison charts, webs that trace logical links, time lines, cause and effect maps, and Venn diagrams to map similarities and differences. The authors of *Classroom Instruction That Works* report that creating graphic representations of ideas is one of the most effective but underused teaching methods.

> *The more we use both systems of representation—linguistic and nonlinguistic—the better we are able to think about and recall knowledge. This is particularly relevant to the classroom, because studies have consistently shown that the primary way we present new knowledge to students is linguistic. We either talk to them about the new content or have them read about the new content. . . . This means that students are commonly left to their own devices to generate nonlinguistic representations.*

When teachers help students in this kind of work, however, the effects on achievement are strong. (Marzano et al. 2001, 73)

Helping students in this kind of work doesn't just mean the teacher putting a diagram on the blackboard. It means engaging the class in figuring out how to diagram a particular concept, giving students practice in mapping ideas, first in groups, and then increasingly as individuals. It means insisting that this is a good thing to do, encouraging them always to try this when they are organizing their thoughts. It means hammering away at it until it becomes a "habit of mind" (Hyerle 2000), until it becomes second nature for your students to reach for a piece of paper and begin sketching a web of ideas.

Educators who write about the value of graphic organizers usually have all students in mind—boys and girls—but the fact that many boys have a special strength in the interpretation of visual, spatially arranged materials makes this methodology an excellent "boy strategy." For some boys, it can be a key for unlocking the mysteries of how thought is formed.

Once students have worked from the ground up, finding the details that might be helpful, then working mindfully to sort out those details, *then* it's time to figure out, like the police detective, a tentative thesis and begin drafting. By this point, it often seems that the essay is ready to write itself and the blank page holds less terror. Kevan Bleach has written about grade 8 boys feeling panic when faced with a difficult writing task, but later agreeing that having "clearly defined steps to follow made the subject more accessible" (1998b, 45).

In this section, I have described steps that, I hope, avoid descending into mere gimmickry, but instead lay bare what happens when people really write. After working through the process, students, including weaker but also some quite able boys and girls, sometimes say, "You know, that really works." Or, as one boy said, "I used to always freeze up when I had to write an essay. I never knew how to start, but now these steps make it seem like something I can do."

Poems: A Guy Thing

Poetry can be an especially tricky problem for boys. In their minds, poetry has feminine associations. You and I know that most published anthologies and most university English courses on poetry are dominated by the work of male poets, but if you ask a teenage boy to picture someone reading poetry, he'll imagine a girl or an effeminate male. Poetry is thought of as being sensitive, which puts it on a collision course with dominant masculine stereotypes.

Interestingly, that prejudice begins to break down when the classroom focus turns to the *writing*, rather than just the reading, of poetry. When they have a chance to actually *do* something with poetry—perform it, dramatize it, and write *lots* of it—boys take greater pleasure in the subject (QCA 1998, 25; Penny 1998, 87).

A simple but successful poetry writing unit can be attached to the study of other literature. The basic strategy is to use published poems as models of how ideas might be treated in a poem, then apply those models to ideas drawn from the core text that we have been studying. Students produce several drafts each day using that day's model, and after a week or so, they have many drafts from which they can choose a few to polish and submit.

For example, after studying *Lord of the Flies* in a grade 10 class, I showed the students a couple of short poems in which the poets focused on an object or a setting. These were poems that I quickly found in available resources. I happened to use "The Tea Shop" by Ezra Pound and "Canadian January Night" by Alden Nowlan, but you'll easily find other pieces like these in your own classroom anthologies. The important feature is that each writer uses a specific object or situation as a springboard for reflection about some aspect of life. (Pound reflects on the poignancy of seeing age foreshadowed in youth; Nowlan reflects on the beauty and terror of harsh Canadian winters.) Then we brainstormed a list of objects mentioned in *Lord of the Flies*—objects that might be similarly used to spark reflections. The list included rocks, the jungle, the lagoon, fire, pigs, sand, sky, sticks and spears, the dead parachutist, and so on. Their homework was to draft at least four poems based on different objects; three objects had to come from the novel, but the fourth could be anything.

Here's a poem that Nick wrote.

The earth is filled with them
Tall and beautiful trees
Green as grass at times
Dark as night at others
But still tall and beautiful
We live because of them
And kill others
With them
A stick is a tree
That has been killed
Killing with that stick
Turns the stick
Into a victim

> *As well as a killer*
> *But still they grow*
> *Tall and beautiful*

Nick normally enjoyed only modest success in English, but I think this is quite a good poem. He plays with paradox and highlights irony with the haunting repetition of "tall and beautiful." The piece builds on the mood and themes of *Lord of the Flies*, where trees at first suggest Eden, then become the dangerous jungle.

Another day, we looked at a piece called "To a Sad Daughter," by Canadian poet Michael Ondaatje. In it, a father enters his daughter's bedroom and sees the possessions she has accumulated; he remembers his hopes for her before she was born, thinks now of what she has become, and leaves her room with a silent wish for the future. I asked students to imagine parents of the surviving boys from Golding's novel entering their sons' rooms and having similar reflections; even the families of the dead boys might enter their rooms and look at the now-empty beds.

Kamal wrote the following poem in the voice of Ralph's mother. (Kamal imagines that Ralph has a souvenir conch in his room; I reminded him that, in the novel, the conch is destroyed on the island, but I suppose Ralph might have made a point of collecting a replacement.)

> *When I step into your room*
> *I see all your shells and that conch that you refuse to talk about.*
> *I hear*
> *the nightly screams that plague your dreams.*
> *If only you'd let me in,*
> *I want to help.*
> *When I first had you*
> *I said to myself, "I'll always be able to help and talk to this one."*
> *I hope you soon learn how to talk to me.*
> *I cry when you're hurt.*

Kamal was a "tough guy," diagnosed with a learning disability, and was struggling in English. (He skipped class for several days when we began reading Shakespeare; when I finally tracked him down, he said it was because he figured he wouldn't like Shakespeare much.) And yet this is a respectable poem, sensitively imagining what might go on between Ralph and his mother after the return home.

Overall, boys did just as well as girls on this project and seemed to find it enjoyable. One boy said this in his cover letter:

*I think my assignment is well done for a person with limited knowledge
in poetry. I enjoyed the subject very much and never thought creating
poems could be this interesting. I wouldn't enjoy poems related to romance
because that doesn't really interest me as much.*

Does it matter? When there are lots of "important" things to learn
in school, why would anyone care that boys were writing poems? It
matters because these boys were paying close attention to things that do
matter, such as the way they can use language to make meaning, the
strangeness of the way beautiful things can be used for evil purposes, and
the loneliness of a parent who realizes that her love for a child isn't
enough to break the wall of silence that separates them. Our lives would
be enriched if more people paid attention to things like that.

The success of this work in engaging boys can be attributed to several
factors.

- The writing was related to a work studied in class. There was an
  option, but no requirement, for some of the poems to be personal.
  It was mainly girls who took advantage of the personal option;
  most boys stayed with the novel, which allowed the treatment of
  feelings to be safely deflected through fictional characters, as in
  Kamal's poem.

- Straightforward models were available, but every day I reminded
  them that they were free to experiment with the models, bending
  them to their own purposes. In other words, the framework was
  there as a guide to be used *mindfully*, not mimicked mechanically.

- There was a tiny hint of competition in my reminder that their
  daily homework was to produce "at least" four or five drafts. I told
  them that published poets always crank out far more drafts than
  they ever end up using, and that they, as students, ought to aim to
  produce as many as possible, even if most end up in the recycling
  bin. A number of boys—some of the most unlikely, nonliterary
  ones—accepted the challenge and came in each day trying to
  outdo their friends in sheer quantity. I know, I know: quality
  matters more than quantity. But it was sure good to see boys
  swaggering in to announce, "I wrote eight poems last night. Beat
  that, if you can!"

Stories: Intergalactic Shoot-Outs

In an entertaining article, Peter Thomas (1997) reflects on the characteristics of narratives written by boys. His title captures the action-

oriented spirit of many male narratives: "Doom to the Red-Eyed Nyungghns from the Planet Glarg." Thomas begins by drawing an analogy between writing and driving.

> *If anything shows the differences between men and women, it is their attitude to cars and driving. Women tend to want safe and comfortable transport. Men like power, instruments and technical options. Younger men, particularly, drive too fast, too assertively, and with too much trust in their own capacities and judgment. . . . I see a similarity in boys' narrative writing. . . . With boys, it's all maximum revs. Each action incident is another gear change and acceleration. It makes for a bumpy journey, with lots of screeching tires, hilltop chases and spectacular crashes. Narrative travel, boy-style, is not restful, and tells us little about the terrain. (24)*

Is Thomas stereotyping male and female drivers and writers? Of course. Is there a strong element of truth in his stereotypes? Absolutely. If you doubt it, ask your car insurance agent about accident statistics for teenage boys, or ask any English teacher who has ever read stories written by grade 9 boys.

The trend starts in early childhood. Young girls at play create scenarios of family life, while boys take their inspiration from television and act out fantasies of the lone superhero, like Batman (Maccoby 1998, 41–42). A research study of grade 7 stories showed that boys were much more likely than girls to use film or television as sources for character and action, and to focus on "an external public world of battle, aggression, retribution" (Gilbert and Gilbert 1998, 212). Of course, the reliance on TV and film, rather than print, for inspiration is hardly surprising, since we also know that boys at that age are far more likely to report doing "very little reading" outside school (Millard 1997, 90). When given a free choice of topics, boys opt to write about "such things as plane crashes, war exploits, and murders, while girls . . . prefer writing which [is] self-reflective or empathetic" (research cited in Millard 1997, 17).

We could shrug this off as a mere difference in style and try, as evaluators of student writing, to develop more of a taste for boys' stories. In fact, however, the differences between boys' and girls' narratives indicate areas where both sexes need to grow. It's fine to enjoy action and there are honorable traditions of thriller, war, catastrophe, and fantasy writing. However, boys who simply transcribe their favorite moments from action movies need to learn that action without feeling, motivation, context, or consequence is *boring*.

The flip side of this problem is also familiar to you if you read teenage girls' writing. Some girls' stories are entirely accounts of inner thoughts and feelings: we find ourselves locked inside a protagonist's head to the point where the reading becomes claustrophobic and airless, and even an author of interior landscapes like Virginia Woolf might cry, "Please, let something *happen* in this story!"

We know the amount of "creative" writing demanded from American students drops off precipitously after the end of the elementary years (Applebee 1993, 162–67). I'm sure that's largely because teachers feel they have to get students ready for the essay-writing demands of college and university, but it may also be partly because they get sick of reading those tales of intergalactic battles (from boys) and solipsistic confessions (from girls). I think, however, we shouldn't give up on the writing of narrative and poetry. It is important to encourage students to be makers of culture themselves, and attempting to master an art yourself is one very good way of learning to appreciate that art when performed by others. Any boy who spends hours practicing guitar or basketball will tell you that that effort makes him better able to appreciate the work of professional musicians or athletes.

The stories written by boys and by girls reveal to us what they are currently able to see and appreciate in stories, and also what they do not yet see or appreciate. By gently pushing them, challenging them to try a bit more, we can help both boys and girls understand more of what happens in writing. One way to push boys to consider character more carefully is to walk them through a process of *character creation*. This can be done in many ways, but one way I have used is based on a visual stimulus—a picture.

I bring in a photograph of a child who has an ambiguous facial expression and is placed in an undefined situation. I tell the class, "This child has an interesting story, but I don't know what that story is. It's going to be your job to imagine it." Students are arranged in random, mixed-sex groups and each given a copy of the picture. They examine it and, with their groups, brainstorm a list of questions they might ask about this picture. ("Who is taking this photo? Why?" "Where is this boy?" "What is that paper in his hand?" "What does the look on his face mean?") Then, still with their groups, they choose a few of their most interesting questions and reach a consensus about possible answers.

Next, they create a personal context for the character: I ask them to think about possible people in this child's life—people who might have something interesting to tell us about him. They agree on roles and each group member prepares a very short monologue (just a few sentences) in which one of those contextual figures gives us a little insight into the figure in the photo. ("I'm Jimmy's aunt, and I remember the time he . . ." "I'm in his class at school, and I can tell you . . ." "I saw that kid on the bus yesterday. . . .") These monologues are read out to the class, so that everyone gets a sense of the range of characters being constructed by other groups.

Finally, it is time for students to write their stories. You might like to do this as a paired- or team-writing activity, but I set them off on their own, telling them that the protagonist in their individual story must be *based* on the character their group has created, but it's their own creation at this point and they should feel free to change details to suit the story they want to tell. I remind them that they have choices of point of view. Will he tell his own story? Will the speaker be one of those other people they created or perhaps a third-person narrator? (Depending on the readiness of your class, you might want to narrow those choices.) I stress that this is a short story: instead of summarizing his whole life, each writer has to choose one episode that will give us a taste of what makes this character interesting.

This assignment isn't a magic fix for the typical boy plot, full of adrenalized action. I still get stories with alien landings and chases in stolen cars, and, in truth, I wasn't trying to eradicate all traces of boys' interests. What the strategy does do, however, is induct students into a way of thinking about stories: thinking about character first and trying to flesh out that character's reality and context before getting engrossed in plot.

Elaboration: Embracing Gibber-Jabber

Anyone who reads student journals is familiar with this phenomenon: many girls seem able to develop and expand their thoughts fluently, while the boys are terse and abrupt. Partly, it's a question of practice. Boys have had much less out-of-school practice at using writing to record their thoughts. In a typical high school classroom, it's likely that at least half the girls have at one time kept their own journals or diaries, and a good chance that most of the boys have never done such a thing (EQAO 2001a).

When my grade 10 students wrote creative add-ons to *Twelfth Night*, Bryan, a struggling student, chose to do a set of "Dear Abby" letters based on the characters in Shakespeare's play. A cover letter is required for all major assignments; in it, the writer must identify strengths and weaknesses in the attached paper. In his cover letter, Bryan wrote:

> *My weakness would defiantly* [sic] *be writing a little shorter than what's needed. I felt it hard to make the letters extensive, even though I left out a little jibber jabber that could have filled a page.*

(It amuses me to imagine that his misspelling of *defiantly* for *definitely* might be a Freudian slip.) It's interesting that Bryan sensed his writing might be "a little shorter than what's needed": there was no official minimum length for the assignment, and at four pages, it surely fit within the normal size for work in that course. His doubt perhaps came from knowing that teachers were always telling him to "elaborate" or "develop" his ideas further, coupled with his sense that he was leaving some things out. He judged his omissions to be not worthwhile, mere "jibber jabber," although there was a worrying possibility that they might be just the kind of thing an English teacher would like.

Indeed, when I read his Dear Abby letters, it was noticeable that Bryan wasn't going much beyond stating the problems that we already knew the characters had; he wasn't trying to work his way into their experience. I pointed that out to Bryan and in my overall comment suggested that he should "let them talk enough about their problems that we get to understand their feelings."

A *general* comment like that, however, wouldn't be enough to let Bryan know what to do in a revision. Students who write stingy, unelaborated prose need to have someone raise *precise* questions about *specific* spots in the writing. Being told to "go into more detail" as an overall comment is something they've heard only too often: if they knew what that meant, they would have done it by now. "Explain yourself" is nothing more than a chant of voodoo pedagogy until it is reworked into specific questions targeted at exact locations in the student's work.

That's why I went through Bryan's paper and found specific phrases to underline and question. For example, Maria marries Toby at the end of *Twelfth Night*, and Bryan had imagined her writing the following complaint:

> *Dear Abby,*
>
> *I have a problem. I am happily married to a wonderful man. The only problem with my husband is his drinking problem. When he is not drinking he's the most wonderful person to be around, but when he is drinking he can be very insensitive. What should I do?*
>
> *Maria*

I underlined "he can be very insensitive" and wrote, "Tell what he does at those times." After seeing my comments, Bryan, in his rewrite, added two sentences at that point:

> *Once he gets drunk all he wants to do is carouse with his friends all night long. He wastes his time with childish pranks and nonsense.*

There were three or four other places like that, where my specific questions prompted changes. Maybe some of these changes were ideas that

Bryan had originally dismissed as being unnecessary. His "just the facts, ma'am" attitude needs to make room for a little of what he thought was gibber-jabber.

I'm reminded of a grade 8 teacher who asked her students to hand in a report on what they did during Spring Break. She was reading responses a page or two in length until she came to one boy's report, which was, in its entirety, one sentence: "I went to New York with my dad." She questioned him the next day and, of course, there were lots of exciting specifics that he could talk about, but it hadn't occurred to him that that's what his teacher wanted to read. After all, she had asked what he did on his break, and he had literally answered her question, hadn't he? If a friend had passed him in the hall and said, "Hey, what did you do last week?" his one-sentence answer would have been exactly right, but there's a specific literacy game—the game of writing about your vacation—that requires more elaboration. Boys in particular don't automatically recognize all the "rules" of the literacy games they're expected to play, especially if no one has thought to make them explicit.

Revising and Editing: A Team Effort

The difficulty, of course, is time—our time. Marking up a paper like Bryan's once isn't going to be enough: Bryan isn't going to have an overnight transformation and say, "Oh, now I see what those English teachers wanted. I'll do it differently from now on." No, Bryan will have to hear these questions many times before he can internalize the dialogue and begin to ask *himself* the questions that an attentive reader might ask. Unless you're a remedial teacher with only five or six students, you can't, all by yourself, do all the questioning necessary to build the scaffolding Bryan needs.

Happily, one solution to that dilemma could be seen right on Bryan's paper. When I compared Bryan's revision with the original, marked-up version, I found not only my queries, but also similar questions in someone else's handwriting. Bryan's mother had taken my cue and raised her own excellent questions that led Bryan to further elaboration. You can't count on all the mothers out there to share your work this way, but you do have to enlist someone's help.

You have a classroom full of students, and they're the ones who must be taught to do this work. Most of us probably use some form of peer editing to get students helping each other, but we need to be sure that we teach them techniques that will make the most difference. The simplest way to do this is to have a teacher-directed lesson in which the whole class works together on one sample piece of writing (photocopied or projected on an overhead screen), followed by a small-group practice run before they begin to work on each other's writing in earnest.

When we're trying to help boys write more elaborated narratives, the student editors have to learn to stand in for the puzzled reader, asking questions that help the writer learn what exactly it means to explain more. In the article about boys' narratives cited earlier, Peter Thomas helpfully identifies three areas where boys are likely to fail to recognize their readers' needs.

- Character motivation may be slight.

- Mood and manner may be absent *or* explicitly asserted, *telling* us the monster was "terrifying" rather than *showing* us terrifying features.

- Conflicts may play out in an amoral universe where struggles are won and lost with little sense of a social or moral context. (1997, 27–30)

For Thomas, *teachers* should be ready to intervene with helpful questions that push students to redraft. I agree, but I also think teaching *students* to ask these questions of their fellow students wins greater gains. That way, your classroom becomes a true writing workshop, full of writers asking each other, "Why is this character acting like that?" "How does she look when she hears that news?" "What makes the monster look so terrifying?" "What's going to happen to him as a person now that he has killed all those people?"

Of course, to help girls move beyond the sealed-up interior narratives that some of them may write, readers need a different set of questions. They need to ask, "Couldn't you bring another character into the story so that we could see her relating to different people?" "Couldn't your protagonist *show* us her feelings by her actions or her looks, instead of your narrator always having to go inside her head?" "You said here she feels 'nervous,' but can you make something happen that will show us that?"

The skills needed for good peer editing must be explicitly taught and the practices must be firmly insisted upon. Without support and vigilance, nothing degenerates into slackness as quickly as peer editing, especially with boys. One high school teacher examined how her students handled peer editing sessions and realized that while girls seemed to be enjoying the collaborative occasion, boys were uncomfortable, making fewer comments to each other and even avoiding the task by working alone, if allowed. She asked students to explain how they felt about peer editing and found that while girls saw it as an opportunity to share in each other's creations, boys saw it as fault-finding and an invasion of their privacy (Styslinger 1999, 54).

This makes good sense in terms of male psychology: boys like to prove that they can do things independently, and they often don't handle public criticism well. Establishing their rank in a hierarchy, their rung on a ladder, seems to be a lifelong project for some boys and men (Maccoby 1998, 38; Gurian 1998, 99). If you see yourself in a competition for status, being told that you made a mistake or could have done something better may be perceived as a put-down, rather than as collaborative support. That makes peer editing a potentially threatening situation to be resisted or treated as shallowly—as safely—as possible.

Here are three suggestions for dealing with this problem.

- Try to have mixed-sex editing partners or groups. Boys' and girls' different styles of writing are likely to complement each other: both can learn from each other. Also, boys may feel less competitively threatened by a female partner.

- Model the review process yourself. Hand out your own writing and ask for hard, constructive criticism from the class. Show them how to handle it. (Think aloud: let them know if someone says something that hurts.) Tell them what you're doing: "I want you to see how a writer deals with this."

- Point out that collaborative criticism is a feature of much creative work. We know that writers have to work with editors, but examples from other media may strike a more resonant chord with boys: recording artists and filmmakers spend a long time working hard to produce polished work, and they learn to value the critical eyes and ears of their cocreators.

Postscript: What About Computers?

Until the recent past, writing meant picking up a pen and scribing by hand. Most of you have probably moved, as I have, to a different world, a post-hand-script world in which most serious writing is generated on computers. The classroom, where the pen is still indispensable, is an almost anachronous vestige of the old world, but that too is changing as computers make their way into schools and into the homes of students.

Some see this development as offering a special ray of hope for boys. We know that boys, on the whole, like computers and are more likely than girls to have and use computers at home (Millard 1997, 153). Of course, liking to work with machines is a classic male trait. In fact, girls' relative lack of interest in computer technology is a worrying problem, with the computer emerging as the new requisite tool of communication. In schools where access to computers is limited, teachers are warned to prevent boys from squeezing girls out of time on the machines. Of course, much of boys' computer time at home is spent on arcade-style games, where the action plays out like the plots in their stories, but, more promisingly, composing on a computer is the one form of writing that seems particularly attractive to boys. When grade 10 students were asked what kinds of writing they regularly did outside of school, the only areas where boys nearly matched girls' writing frequency were the two computer-based forms: email and Internet chat room discussions (EQAO 2001a). I've seen plenty of "unacademic" or "nonverbal" boys become unblocked when they get their hands on a keyboard. They'll tell you, "I love writing on the computer." At the simplest level, writing becomes a much more rewarding experience for them. Boys notoriously have messier handwriting than girls, and the computer eliminates mess: their writing *looks* good, right from the beginning.

It is therefore tempting to say, "Let's get boys writing on computers as much as possible." For a few years, I was lucky enough to teach some of my classes in a room full of computers. It was a good experience for both boys and girls, but I'm not sure it was indispensable, and it is not a panacea that I can endorse without reservations. Politicians promise computers in every classroom the way they used to promise a chicken in every pot, but computers, like any educational tool, have to be used intelligently by teachers and students who understand both the capabilities and the limitations of their tools.

Some recent research warns that computer use may actually work against the best interests of students (Freedman and St-Martin 2000). For example, the computer makes correction at the surface level easy, and a number of researchers are noticing that students composing on computers concentrate on that level of surface fix, sometimes neglecting overall organization and the more substantial recasting that would count as real revision. We know it's dangerous to get caught up in picky proofreading too early in the writing process, but word-processing software that identifies spelling and grammar errors as you type creates exactly that distraction. At the very least, students should be told to turn off the automatic spellcheck until they're finished drafting. Beyond that, they still need solid, insistent instruction on how good writing demands shaping. The computer certainly makes it technically easier to do heavy-duty revision *once you understand what that revision could be*, but it doesn't teach how or why to rework your writing beyond the sentence-level corrections of spelling and grammar software. Cutting and pasting chunks of text is easy on a computer, *but you still need to be taught why you'd want to cut and paste anything.*

These researchers have also noted the isolating, hypnotic effect of the computer screen. Students writing on computers are much less likely to confer with the teacher and students around them. In other words, "Students writing entirely by computer were actually exposed to less of a process approach in their classes—despite the intentions of their teachers" (244). This is particularly dangerous for boys, who may already have a tendency to isolate themselves when writing and avoid or pay only lip service to collaborative editing processes, as I pointed out earlier. One way of countering this difficulty would be to use the computer for *collaborative* writing tasks. Two, three, even four students may be able to gather comfortably around one monitor. This is more convenient for a group than trying to see one piece of paper lying flat on a table, and a collaborative task should produce more genuine think-aloud discussion about the writing.

As you see, these reservations don't close the door on computer use, but they do mean that teachers have to think carefully about what's happening when students write with word-processing software. Specifically, we have to *think* about *thinking*: we have to think about what's going on inside students' minds when they write, and we have to ask ourselves what ought to be going on if they are to learn how to think like writers.

But, of course, thinking—mindfulness—has been the theme of this whole chapter. The skill of writing is a skill of thinking—thinking that has sometimes been shrouded by a voodoo veil of secrecy, despite teachers' best intentions. There are boys and girls who need to see the veil drawn back, just as Dorothy's dog pulls back the curtain that had concealed the wizard at the end of *The Wizard of Oz*. Once the veil is lifted and they can see the true machinery of thought and writing, students have a chance of taking that machinery into their own hands.

6 *I Have Better Things to Do*

Reading

Jeffrey Wilhelm describes a classroom incident in which a capable student—a girl—is taunted with the accusation that she has been reading at home. One boy jeers, "If you have nothing better to do at home than read you'd better think about getting a real life" (1997, 21). In his study of grade 8 students, Kevan Bleach quotes an all-too-typical boy:

> *I don't read much . . . I do what I have to do and no more . . . It's an effort to pick up a book and read page after page . . . I have better things to do. (1998b, 41)*

In class one day, I happened to mention an initiative in Tennessee to supply each preschool child with a small library of children's books, and one of my fifteen-year-old male students was disgusted: "They give them *books*?" he said. For him, that was a pathetic gift to be giving a child.

When we're addressing the issue of boys' *writing*, English teachers have one big advantage. There are plenty of credible male role models for writing: songwriters, scriptwriters, news reporters, magazine writers, speech writers, businessmen preparing reports, novelists, and indeed the authors of most books on the shelves of any bookstore. There's no problem convincing kids that writing is something that guys do.

When we turn to *reading*, however, we have arrived at the front line of the literacy battleground. It is here that resistance is the most entrenched. Teachers know that one of the very best ways of becoming a good writer is to do lots of reading: we see reading and writing as being inseparably married. For many boys, however, reading and writing are irreconcilably divorced. Writing is something you *do*: it's an activity, it's productive, it influences others to see things your way, and it can make you rich and famous. Reading, on the other hand, seems passive and lonely. You go off by yourself and just sit there. You're not having a good time with your friends, you're not being physically active, and if you actually *like* it, well, then you're willingly doing something that lots of other guys only do when forced by a teacher. You're wasting your time with something that girls may enjoy, only because they don't have anything better to do. If a guy wins a *writing* contest, he may earn grudging respect from his peers, but if he's an eager *reader*, he'll more likely win pity or contempt.

Against that entrenched attitude, we stand with our certain knowledge that if students read only what they are forced to read for school, they'll never become really good readers. U.S. Department of Education statistics confirm that students who read "for fun"—even if it's only monthly—score higher on reading tests than students who say they never read for fun. Particularly worrying is the finding that the percentage of thirteen- and seventeen-year-olds who read for fun on a daily basis has decreased since 1984. For that matter, when kids of those ages are asked how much reading they see their *parents* doing—which also correlates with student success—that amount has also fallen in the past two decades (NCES 2000, 76–78).

Although reading is always less popular with boys, if a boy has a chance of being a dedicated reader, it is more likely to be during his preadolescent years. We would like to think that a reading habit developed early in life would stick with a boy, and that's probably true for many, but the research cited previously suggests that there is a falling-off of pleasure reading during early adolescence, that is, during the middle school and secondary years. A similar pattern appears in Britain, where there is a noticeable decline in voluntary reading around age fourteen. That decline appears in both boys and girls, but the drop in boys' reading has become more pronounced in the past thirty years (Hall and Coles 1997, 62–64).

We can point to a link between pleasure reading and reading scores, but the real importance of pleasure reading isn't just about boosting scores on someone's test. It's about a vision of what it means to be a whole person, a person whose life and imagination are enriched by reading more than instruction manuals and stock market quotes, a person whose reading of life is informed by reading authors who have written searchingly of the human condition. It may sometimes seem that the tests have taken over, but I don't think many of us became English teachers because we wanted to prepare kids to write tests. We became English teachers because we believed that the world of books matters and that reading changes lives. We believe that an education isn't just a stockpiling of data but an enlargement of our ability to imagine a world. For those reasons, we have to be gravely concerned when we find that many of our students do not read for pleasure.

Personal Reading Time

There's plenty of competition for students' time, including part-time jobs, television, computer games, and, in recent years, the Internet. (Time spent on the Internet does include reading, although it doesn't usually show up in "pleasure reading" statistics. The quality of online reading experiences varies widely, of course.) In a case study of one British secondary school, students were questioned about the decrease in their independent reading. Predictably, they cited "the pressures of coursework and a more active social life" as reasons, but students also pointed out that, *in earlier grades, they had regular personal reading time in class, with some kind of record-keeping that allowed teachers to monitor the quantity of their reading.* When that time and accountability disappear in the secondary years, so does, for many students, the reading habit (QCA 1998, 14). Although that report comes from the United Kingdom, I'm sure we see exactly the same effect on this side of the Atlantic. I've heard plenty of senior students lament, "I used to do lots of reading in elementary school, but now we're so busy and they don't give us time to read things that *we* want to read."

I can imagine teachers protesting, "In high school, we have a pile of course content to cover. We can't use class time just for letting them read anything they want. Shouldn't they have developed their own reading habits by the time they're fifteen?" Yes, I suppose they should have, but it seems they haven't. Boys' commitment to the idea of reading as a pleasure always was flimsier than girls', and when the pressure and support for personal reading disappear in secondary school, large numbers of boys simply haven't developed the dedication to keep them going at the habit.

We face an overload of curriculum expectations and demands that we prepare students for external tests. In that hard-nosed achievement race, it's difficult to find time for something that seems so indulgent as reading for fun, and we end up paying only lip service to the idea of pleasure reading.

It's a pity. We know there's a growth spurt in boys' brains, on average, around age fifteen. This spurt causes a "refinement of abstract thinking, a prerequisite for mature and reflective thought" (Newberger 1999, 256): around ages fourteen to sixteen, boys develop much more "intellectual minds" (Gurian 1998, 121). They are suddenly ready for new ideas and new ways of thinking, hungry for material that would allow them to try out their new turbocharged brains. Those brains are receptive grounds for fresh, more mature kinds of reading.

But what do teachers do at that point in their students' development? In effect, many of us say, "There's no more time in school for you to be pursuing your own reading interests. That was fine when you were younger, but now we have more important things to do." That confirms exactly what those boys always suspected: that there *are* better things to do than reading.

I include personal reading time in grade 9 and 10 courses: one out of every four classes is a reading period. I tell them this time is precious: I promise that I will never steal it away from them. That means that no matter how interesting or how unfinished the work we are doing today, it will never spill over into tomorrow if tomorrow is reading period. Nothing is more important than reading time. Ten minutes before the end of reading period, they stop and write quick reports on what they read that day. This allows me to check that they actually were reading, and I can offer encouragement or suggestions for further reading.

What about grades 11 and 12? There, I confess, the sheer number of works to be covered makes it impractical to include so much class time for personal reading, but by then students are also assigned independent study projects that can be truly tailored to individual tastes, allowing students to apply academic tools of research and analysis to reading material of their own choice. The message can still be that it's important to work through one's own interests in reading.

The reading preferred by boys is often different from that preferred by girls or chosen by English teachers for class study. Depending on the age, boys may choose fantasy, action stories, and nonfiction, including biographies of sports stars and adventurers, and magazines about sports, cars, and computers. At younger ages, joke books are popular. At a school book sale, I watched the somewhat worn-looking mother of a ten-year-old desperately trying to find something that her son might like to read, while he loudly declared his sole interest: "Joke books! That's what I want. Do they have any joke books here?" Even up to grades 9 and 10, some boys will bring joke books and *Mad Magazine*s to reading periods; in my experience, girls never bring that kind of material.

Some of you might prefer to limit the list of approved reading, and you might be right to do so, but, short of pornography or hate literature, I don't exclude anything. I figure if I'm going to tell them it's important to find things they genuinely want to read, I had better mean what I say and respect their choices. I can always look for openings where I might suggest other possibilities, but there may be a huge gap between the English teacher's idea of good reading and the reluctant reader's idea. There is some evidence, for example, that the early adolescent novels, often used in middle schools as a way of introducing students to "relevant" fiction—social realism about gangs, bullying, and so on—are *not*, in fact, what the reluctant male reader would choose himself as interesting reading (Millard 1997, 129).

To gain maximum benefit from a personal reading program, *it is crucial that there be sharing time or a "book talk" component*: some way for kids (and teacher) to hear what other people are enjoying reading. The way you handle this will vary, depending on what seems right for you and your students. You might have a few people each day reporting on what they are reading, or you might have monthly sessions where everyone briefly describes "the best thing I've read in the past month," or you might have small-group reading circles for them to chat about their reading. If they are studying books as part of an independent study, there may be a short oral report to the class.

Why is it so important that some form of book chat be implemented? When kids are asked how they discover good books to read, hearing about books from friends or female family members turns out to be a *major resource* for girls. Boys, on the other hand, *almost never* recommend books to each other (Millard 1997, 211; Penny 1998, 301; QCA 1998, 11). It makes sense, after all: reading isn't seen as a legitimate masculine pastime, so it can be nearly impossible for a guy to say to his friends, "Can you recommend any good books for me?" That means that, unlike girls, boys don't build up a network of book-sharing friends and don't see themselves as part of a community of readers. We, the teachers, have to create those communities in our classrooms, modeling book talk and setting in place routines of sharing—routines that would not spontaneously evolve without our intervention.

That all sounds pretty positive, but I must temper my enthusiasm. It is easy to be disappointed by the results of personal reading programs. When we invite students to read what they want to read, the instinctive response of many boys is that they don't want to read anything. In *Differently Literate*, Elaine Millard reports on an open-ended survey of Grade 7 boys' reading choices: the survey predictably revealed a preference for action stories, but an even bigger preference for nothing at all, with over a third of the boys declining to name anything as favorite reading (1997, 53). The practical result of this is that, on reading period days, boys are more likely to show up with hastily chosen reading to which they have no real commitment, or without any reading material at all. They will be the ones who "forget" to bring a book or magazine, relying on a book grabbed from the classroom supply. Sometimes I've made a quick, lucky match of book and student from materials at hand; at other times, I'm sure the student just goes through the uncommitted motions of reading. These students are wasting an important opportunity, and that worries me, but I have to remind myself that it's only a small number of students who opt out this way. Most students use the time well, and we'd never do anything in school if we insisted on a 100 percent success rate.

Even once there are books in everyone's hands, we shouldn't be unrealistic about the growth we're expecting. Many students—boys and girls—go through long stretches of time reading only one narrow type of material. It doesn't always happen that the boy who is reading *Mad Magazine* at the beginning of the year will be reading Hemingway by the end of the year. As Elaine Millard points out, a reading curriculum based on pupils' private choice can result in both sexes experiencing only "a limited range of genre that reinforces attitudes, rather than widens experience" (162). In particular, if we understand that a central project for adolescence is development of the self, and if we believe that literature's portrayal of characters can speak to that development, then we can't help noticing that girls' choice of reading—fiction with more emphasis on character development and psychological complexity—is going to be a bigger help with identity development than the joke books or computer articles that boys may choose (130). (Conversely, it might be useful for girls to develop more of a taste for computer magazines, if they're not going to be disadvantaged in a high-tech economy.)

If we want to win the reluctant readers, we can't be elitist and insist that students read only capital L literature. However, student-chosen reading, even with the support of a rich classroom culture of book talk, will take us only so far. It doesn't make a whole curriculum. It's a valuable part of a reading program, but there comes a point when there is a role for the teacher as mediator, bringing books and kids together—books that they might never have chosen for themselves—and actively teaching reading strategies that make it possible for those kids and those books to connect.

Voodoo Secrets of Reading

I began Chapter 5 by telling the story of Oliver wanting to know how to go about writing a poem. After that episode, I went on to wonder what other secrets we might be neglecting to share with our students and realized that reading—especially reading the way English teachers want you to—can seem equally mysterious, especially to boys.

A senior student, reflecting on his own reading, wrote:

> *I've never really thought about it before. I always knew that people had opinions on certain subjects that differed from mine. Take a poem for instance. Some students, the majority being female, are always able to find the "deeper meaning" of a poem. The guys, on the other hand, almost always take the poem for face value and never give it a second thought.*

There's a value judgment being made by those boys—they don't think poetry deserves "a second thought"—but this student also puts his finger on feelings of inadequacy: there's some power those girls have to see things that are hidden from the guys. This plugs into powerful stereotypes about female intuition and women's annoying expectation that men will understand things that have been left unspoken. To some men, more comfortable with the literal and the explicit, it seems that both poems and women expect you to read between the lines. What teachers see as subtlety or implication sometimes gets translated in boys' minds into a blind hunt for secret messages and the perverse notion that literature has hidden meanings. What kind of nutty person would try to *hide* meaning? Why can't they just come out and *tell* you what they mean?

Just as some students need to see how writing happens, some need to hear how reading happens, moment-by-moment. In classrooms, we do lots of things *after* reading is *finished*. Students write responses, analyze symbolism, and answer questions, but that's not the same as talking about reading, any more than doing an autopsy on a dead body gives you a sense of what it was like to dance and sing with the living person. It doesn't necessarily help the poor kid who couldn't see it in the first place, the kid who comes to you and says, "I don't get it. Some people seem to be able to see things in books, but I never see it until someone explains it to me."

In *Reshaping High School English* (1997), I described a number of general habits of good readers, habits that students can be taught and can practice. When these reading activities are made explicit through think-alouds and other forms of classroom instruction, poorer readers suddenly have a chance to see these secret habits and try them out for themselves.

I'll briefly reiterate those habits here, then, in the next section, turn to the special difficulties and strengths that boys can bring to reading. (For a different but compatible approach to reading strategies, see Wilhelm, Baker, and Dube's *Strategic Reading* [2001].)

- *Good readers travel through a text, in an experience that unfolds over time.* We move through the landscape of a text, beginning with expectations and predictions that change as we pass through the changing scenery, and gradually get a clearer idea of where we're going and where we have been. The reader at the end of the journey has a particular vantage point, but arriving at that understanding is only a later part of the experience. Sometimes weak readers hear seasoned travelers' reports of what books look like by the end, when what they really needed was help getting through earlier stages of the journey.

- *Good readers often visualize what they are reading.* Some of us are more visual than others, but many good readers *see* the world of the book in a way that allows them to enter imaginatively into that world.

- *Good readers make connections, not only within the text but also to experiences outside the text, including other literary and nonliterary texts, and to their own lives.* Making connections is a cornerstone of our thinking: it is the way we make sense of everything. Whenever we encounter something new, we try to figure out how it might be like or unlike previous experiences, try to fit it into a larger structure of understanding. I should say, we draw connections *if* we are making rich meaning. The poor learner, on the other hand, drifts from event to event and sees few relationships between them. Poor readers just see one word after another, one darned book after another.

- *Good readers fit ideas together into patterns that can often be expressed spatially.* We begin to see patterns of connection, clusters of characters and events that fit together or sort themselves out into triangles, webs, flowcharts, and hierarchies.

- *Good readers learn to fill in inferential gaps.* A text can't and doesn't *need* to say everything, and we learn to read the shorthand of stories. When we read, "She quickly turned away," we understand that this isn't just a physical stage direction, but that it shows something about the character's feelings.

- *Good readers notice and critically question the silences of a text.* A text can't and doesn't *want* to say everything. Every writer has his or her favored topics, and this necessitates leaving out what that writer judges to be distractions. Examining what counts as important and what gets dismissed as irrelevant can reveal a lot about writers and their work. It also reveals a lot about the culture that gives birth to these works. This kind of critical reading has been relatively uncommon in schools in the past, except in studies of popular culture and the media, or in feminist analysis of the omissions in canonical texts.

Each habit can be singled out for demonstration and practice in class. To take the first habit as an example, we can build up a sense of things changing over time by focusing on the predictions we make while reading. Every primary teacher knows that making predictions is an essential reading strategy. Before they turn the page in a storybook, they ask, "What do you think is going to happen when she goes through that door?" In the secondary schools, some of us have forgotten about predicting. Maybe we never knew it: most of us weren't trained as reading teachers. As a result we have sometimes dumped whole books into kids' laps without teaching about predicting your way through these more mature texts, and for some of those kids, it was just a bewildering pile of words.

We can stop after the first part of a story, even sometimes after the first few lines or words, and get kids talking about the predictions they make at those points and explaining the reasons for those predictions. Their forecasts don't have to be "right." Sometimes authors sucker us in and create clever surprises, but you don't enjoy the pleasure of the surprise unless you've played along and made the predictions. Some poor readers maybe can't predict much, but classroom talk can lay bare *how* that thinking happens, and they can listen and start to internalize it, and maybe at the next stop they'll be able to predict something.

None of these reading practices can be digested in a one-shot lesson; each needs lots of practice and reinforcement. A grade 10 class and I had been working hard for about a month on making connections. I told them, "This is what good readers do," and for everything we read, we brainstormed what it reminded us of and what those links meant. They wrote journals about the connections they saw; they talked in small groups and made presentations about connections. We made a fetish of connections because I wanted it to be so habitual that they couldn't read a shopping list without asking themselves what it reminded them of.

Then we moved on from that phase. One day, some weeks later, we read a poem in class. It was about poetry being like deep-sea diving and finding treasure. Everett—a very weak student—suddenly put up his hand.

"Sir, can I please make a connection?"

"Well sure, Everett."

"Sir, here's my connection. This poem sounds to me like a travel brochure where they make it sound like a great vacation."

"Ah, that's interesting. Can you take that any further?"

He couldn't make much more of it right then, and other students continued the discussion, until suddenly Everett's hand went up again.

"Sir, that's it! It's like you're being sold on this great vacation, and if you just go into the poet's world, it'll be like a wonderful cruise and you'll have a good time and find something really valuable and everything."

Everett was radiant with pride and excitement, because he'd "gotten" a poem. After years of watching other people get things out of their reading, Everett had finally seen something himself.

Notice that I don't deserve credit for teaching *that poem*. What I did was hammer away at connection making—a reading and thinking strategy—until it was almost second nature for the class, including Everett. Making those strategies habitual puts reading power into the hands of students like Everett, who need a "how-to-read" approach to literature.

Sometimes—more in the past than now—I have been the one who spelled out specific "how-to-read" strategies. If we were doing poetry, for example, I might have written on the blackboard a short list of Mr. Pirie's Rules and Reminders for Reading Poetry. The list would include tips like these:

- Poems are an especially concentrated form of language and must be read over several times, *slowly*.
- Sound is important: read the poem *aloud*, or at least say the words in your head.
- *Endings* are important: pay special attention to closing lines.
- Pay attention to *repetitions*: they aren't accidental.

Of course, the title of this list was tongue-in-cheek, and I wouldn't use the word *rules* if I didn't think they would catch the joke. Our goal is to teach reading mindfully and flexibly, which means we don't want to encourage formulaic reading any more than we want to see formulaic writing. That's why Mr. Pirie's final "rule" was always:

- Remember that really there are no rules for reading poetry.

There's still sometimes room for that style of teacher-directed instruction, but in recent years I've become more interested in seeing students themselves generate strategies. Now when we embark on the reading of a complex, challenging novel (or poem, story, or play), I pose this as our central question throughout the study: *"What does a reader have to be able to do in order to make rich meaning of this text?"* You'll notice that that's a radically different question from the one that was traditionally at the center of a literature class: "What does this text mean?" We still talk about that question, of course, but we keep coming back to the "how-to" question, which breaks down to several specific questions, any one of which could be material for extended study. "What might we be paying attention to here?" "What connections might we be drawing?" "What predictions are we making? Why?" "How do we handle a contradiction?" "What different kinds of questions might we be asking ourselves as we read, and do certain questions lead us down more interesting paths than others?" Throughout these sessions, I insist that there is more than one good or useful way to approach reading: we are comparing notes, looking for help from each other, but not imagining that we're going to find the one right way of reading.

In *The Teaching Gap* (1999), James Stigler and James Hiebert analyze the teaching being done in grade 8 mathematics classes in Japan, Germany, and the USA. Distinct patterns of instruction emerge, with a particularly striking contrast between American and Japanese teachers. In American classrooms, the teacher typically leads the class through a demonstration of how to solve a problem or perform a particular operation; then the students practice the routine by solving many problems that follow the same pattern. In Japan, the teacher is more likely to pose a new problem, *then ask the students to find possible ways of solving that problem*. It is made clear to students that many different approaches are possible.

Stigler and Hiebert point out that one may ask, "Who is doing real mathematical work in these lessons?" In the American classrooms, the teacher presents a procedure, which is then practiced by the students only as an already-established routine. In Japanese classrooms, the students are more likely to be involved in the process of mathematical inquiry, developing procedures and concepts, *figuring out for themselves* possible ways of going at the material. They're the ones doing real mathematics. As a result, according to Stigler and Hiebert, Japanese students achieve greater depth of mathematical understanding.

When I apply those insights to reading instruction in the English program, I think I am confirmed in being cautious about simply delivering a prepackaged set of strategies to students. To paraphrase Stigler and Hiebert's question, we could ask, "Who is doing the most thinking about reading processes in this classroom?" The answer should be "The students." That doesn't mean that the teacher can't deliver a think-aloud demonstration of how he or she reads a passage. It does mean that such a demonstration has to be delivered tentatively, as one possible way of reading, mindful of other possibilities, capitalizing on what students already know and can teach each other. Making the reading process explicit doesn't mean that the teacher delivers a *quick-step reading gimmick*; it ought to mean that *students* work at making explicit *for themselves and for each other* how reading happens. A "how-to" approach to reading strategies should make clear that "how to read" is a rich field of study, worthy of years of effort by the students themselves, not a foolproof trick that the teacher can hand over in three easy lessons. Reading isn't an impenetrable mystery—it's not voodoo—but it's also not an "Easy-Bake" recipe.

In an article titled "You Can't Play If You Don't Know the Rules," Frederick Hamel and Michael Smith describe lessons designed to help students in a connection-making activity. The key steps are getting students to make clear exactly how they read popular forms like comics and then *connecting* that skill with the reading of literary narrative. This is "instruction that makes interpretive strategies explicit," with the teacher's primary role being to "encourage students to explain how they went about their journey" (1998, 359). As those strategies become explicit, they can be applied to increasingly sophisticated material. Hamel and Smith describe the success of this approach with "lower-track" students, who are "often unsure of the moves that good readers make" (375). We know that many of those lower-track students will be boys. I must add, however, that this is an approach that I use in all levels of reading instruction, whether the material be *The Outsiders* with a lower-track class or a Victorian novel in the hands of gifted senior students. The idea of turning literature study into a practical "how-to" investigation of the reading process makes instinctive good sense to boys at all levels. They like to figure out how things work, and they like to learn how to *do* things.

Sometimes when people talk about how to educate boys, they begin *and end* with the observation that boys have their own preferred reading and respond well to particular kinds of questions. Some educators are quick to say, "Shouldn't we change the reading to include more of those things that they like to read?" The next step in this line of thinking is sometimes, "Let's also give them more short-answer, fact-oriented questions on their reading; they handle that better." Although, as I said earlier, personal reading for pleasure has an important place in the English program, to go no further than that would be a dreary surrender to the status quo. Boys don't need us to give up on them, merely to let them continue doing what they can already do. Boys do like to learn and they are happy to gain new kinds of textual power. The hostility that some boys hold for reading comes from several sources, but part of it is defensive: a suspicion that literary reading is a trick that girls instinctively understand better than boys do, and a fear of looking stupid if they try to play that game. We can be mediators between boys and a richer world of reading if we're willing to help them find out how it's done.

Exploding Cows: The Great Divide

Every now and then in class, something unexpected happens that helps me piece together larger chunks of the puzzle of boys in English. The story I'm going to tell you now is, on the surface, about watching television, but you'll see that it's really about a quality of boys' thinking—a difference that has implications for the way we teach reading.

My grade 10 class had finished working on Golding's *Lord of the Flies*. We understood that, in Golding's view, violence is deeply rooted in human nature. As we moved on to our media studies unit, I wanted to hold on to that theme and have them consider the handling of violence in contemporary media. I decided to show the class a five-minute animated video called *Watching TV* (1994). This video assaults the viewer with a deluge of cartoon violence: cows explode, glass shatters, and cartoon figures are murdered, all with breathtakingly fast editing. The film was produced with the assistance of a family violence prevention group and is intended to make us question our acceptance of violent amusements. Spending huge portions of our lives watching TV, we are immersed in just such a bloody flood of images and eventually come to see it all as entertainment. In this cartoon, news stories about terrorist atrocities cut to action movies, which cut to an ominous commercial for a Ladyslayer shaver. Some images are sinister, while others come from the two-dimensional world of Roadrunner cartoons.

Adapting an idea from the accompanying teacher's guide, I had students record their responses, moment-by-moment, on a sheet of paper divided into three sections. In the top third, they were instructed to place a check mark every time they found an image in the video disturbing. In the bottom third, they would place a mark if they ever found an image amusing. The middle of the page was for checks when a violent image appeared, but left them feeling neutral. There are enough violent acts in the cartoon that everyone would have dozens of check marks somewhere on his or her page by the end of five minutes. In the follow-up discussion, we would compare notes about our reactions.

This class was a "good" grade 10 class, full of decent, friendly, co-operative kids. Everyone was passing the course. Like many students at this age, when they chose their seats on the first day of school, they had spontaneously segregated themselves: all the boys on one side of the room and all the girls on the other.

As soon as the video began, it became obvious that there was a split between the responses of the two sides of the room. The boys found almost every image funny. Of course, when you're with an audience, laughter builds contagiously, and by the end, all those boys had probably had the most enjoyable five minutes of their day. I particularly noticed Larry, a sensitive, thoughtful boy, who was nearly hysterical: he had to hold his belly to keep it from hurting from so much laughing.

And on the girls' side of the room? Stony silence. As the video went on, several of them seemed increasingly appalled, not so much by the video but by the boys' reaction. Girls began glancing away from the television screen in order to watch the boys in disbelief.

When the tape finished, everyone counted up the check marks he or she had made on the page in front of him or her. *Every single boy had found more than twenty images funny.* (Actually, they were probably laughing so hard that they couldn't keep up with the task of making the check marks.) *Not one of the girls had found more than five images funny; most found none funny.*

I never expect every individual boy or girl to fit neatly into a gender category. As I pointed out in Chapter 2, lots of boys have some attitudes traditionally associated with women, and an even larger portion of girls share conventionally masculine values. I didn't expect to see such an absolute schism between the sexes as I now faced in that room. During the viewing, there may have been an unspoken pressure toward conformity: just as the boys couldn't help sharing each other's laughter, girls may have taken their cue from the other girls. In other words, the results might have been different if students had watched the video alone, without having responses cued by their peers of the same sex. Even a more scattered seating arrangement might have broken up the uniformity of the polarized responses.

There was something here that needed to be talked about. I told the class how surprised I was to see such an absolute division between the two sexes and that I'd like to hear what they thought was behind that difference. As we talked, it became clear that there were two opposed styles of thinking.

For the boys, the film wasn't "real." As Larry said, "If I saw a real person being shot on the street, or a cow being tortured, of course I'd be horrified. But this wasn't real. It's obviously all fake. It's a cartoon. It's just drawings, and the whole thing is so exaggerated that you can't help laughing. How could you not laugh?" he added, turning in genuine puzzlement to the girls in the room.

Christine replied, "But when I see those scenes, I think of the reality that's behind them. People do get shot and killed. That's real, and it's not funny." Other girls nodded in agreement.

Larry countered, with evident frustration, *"But this video isn't real.* It doesn't look at all like real violence."

"I know the video isn't real," Christine pressed on. "But it *reminds* me of the real thing, and when I'm making that connection in my head, how could I possibly find it funny? And why would anyone make an image that reflects reality if they didn't want you to think about the real thing?"

Several other students restated these positions in their own words, but eventually the two sides of the room could only stare at each other, genuinely baffled. Each had heard the other side's thinking, but that thinking seemed to have no point of connection to what they had experienced themselves.

I tried to summarize for them what I had heard them say. "These are two different ways of looking at it. The boys are separating things out. They're saying there's reality on one side and fiction on the other, and those are two separate things that shouldn't be confused. The girls, on the other hand, are connecting things. They say that when they see a fiction, they connect it with reality. I wonder why we have those differences in the way we see this video?"

Several of the girls muttered, "Because the boys are immature. They're insensitive."

The boys didn't take that bait. They probably sensed that they had wandered into a dangerous area where they might find themselves in a gender war of words that they wouldn't win. They've heard men be called insensitive before, and they didn't know how to answer the charge. Instead, I spoke for them.

"Wait a minute," I said. "What the boys are saying isn't really immature or insensitive, is it? I mean, this *is* just a cartoon. It's not immature to insist that there's a difference between fiction and reality, is it?" Turning to the boys, I continued, "And maybe you think the girls are just being too sensitive for thinking about the reality, but they're right too, aren't they? Why would you make an image if you didn't want to remind people of the real thing?"

We went on to talk about specific images that had been disturbing or funny. This was a good enough bunch of students that they were able to listen carefully to differing opinions. I doubt if anyone changed his or her initial response to the video, but at least they could listen to each other with puzzled respect.

We had all glimpsed a very wide chasm that lay between the sexes.

Compartmentalization

What we had seen that day was a fundamental feature of male thinking: the tendency to compartmentalize. By that, I mean the urge to *classify* experience into separate compartments and then *focus narrowly* on each detached fragment *in isolation*, as if it were truly disconnected from its context. For those boys, there were two boxes: one box labeled "fiction" and the other "reality." The video we watched unmistakably belonged in the "fiction" box, and once you've put something into that box, it seems ridiculous to treat it as if it were in the "reality" box.

The girls hadn't made that move in their thinking. Of course they understood that you *could* put the video into a box labeled "fiction," but that didn't define their way of dealing with it. For them, fiction and reality had a more fluid, intermingling, connected relationship.

If boys make a strict distinction between fact and fiction, the usual English program runs into a tricky problem, because those boys also typically see facts as real learning or the important stuff, while the English curriculum is packed with fiction. Nonfiction figures prominently in boys' preferred reading. Of course, it's not quite that simple, because many boys also enjoy reading science fiction and fantasy. Interestingly, those are forms of fiction that make no pretense of being "real." They preserve and even strengthen the division between story and real life, unlike the "realistic" fiction that girls and schools often prefer—stories that deliberately blur the line between fiction and ordinary reality. It seems that for some male readers, if they're going to have fiction, they want it to be pure. Stories that start looking too much like real life are boring, and it can be annoying when teachers talk about characters as if they were real people.

English teachers often start with the assumption that when we're studying literature, we're also studying life, an assumption that may seem soft-headed to a person who has sealed off fiction into its own compartment. Boys who enjoy fantasy and sci fi often enter wholeheartedly into those imaginative worlds, but their pleasure is not at all based on any delusion that the stories are real. "It's just a book," they will contemptuously inform a girl who gets too caught up in a story.

Incidentally, you may also have noticed boys priding themselves on building up an astonishing mastery of trivia from a favorite fantasy writer, stockpiling the facts of the fiction—details that seem irrelevant or distracting to a reader more interested in realistic character analysis or social commentary. ("How many meganeutrons does it take to fuel a Quasi M-39B Hypershuttle?") In other words, they have a taste for facts even in their fiction—not the facts of psychological reality, but little bits of data or factoids that they can swap with their friends like baseball cards.

Fiction and reality aren't the only concepts that lend themselves to strict compartmentalization. Logic versus emotion and masculinity versus femininity are other obvious pairs that can be either connected or polarized, treated as overlapping, intermingling concepts, or locked into separate cells. We noted in Chapter 2 that girls are more likely than boys to embrace some of the traditional values of the other sex, which suggests that boys see a more strictly policed boundary between male and female attributes. Historically, women have been relatively willing to take up "men's work"—more willing than men have been to do "women's work," which doesn't fit the little box labeled "masculine."

In *Women's Ways of Knowing*, Mary Field Belenky and her coauthors identify "connected knowing" as a crucial feature of sophisticated female thought. Many of the college women they interview see a special value in that sort of thinking: "They want to avoid what they perceive to be a shortcoming in many men—the tendency to compartmentalize thought and feeling, home and work, self and other" (1997, 137). In *Understanding the Boys*, John Head sees this urge to compartmentalize as a key characteristic of boys, and he links it to boys' belief in rules (1999, 49). After all, a classification system, whether in botany, in the arts, or in relationships, is a system of rules. Rules help to control chaos, which is exactly the benefit of classification. The problem is that life may not have read the rulebook that we keep writing for it. Reality has an annoying habit of throwing up exceptions that violate our categories: mammals that act like fish, men with feminine strengths, and fictions that are all too real.

Compartmentalization isn't a bad way of thinking, but it's not the only way, and it's not the most useful kind of thinking for every situation. In the English classroom in particular, there are times when it can be highly valued, but many other times when it needs to be complemented by "connected knowing." In the rest of this chapter, I'll consider the implications of this insight for our teaching of reading. As you will see, I first discuss ways in which boys can be led to more connected thinking. Later, I will turn the tables and show how we can honor and reap the benefits of compartmentalized thinking.

Making Connections

I have suggested that making connections needs to be explicitly taught as a reading strategy, but we might ask exactly which kinds of connections are and are not being made. After all, it's not that boys never make any connections at all: they'd never learn anything if that were the case. It is rather that there are particular patterns of connection and disconnection characteristic of boys. We want to take advantage of those patterns when we can, and we also want to help boys grow and become more flexible and able to make other, less familiar connections.

A study of 120 "learning logs" (or reading response journals) from sixteen- and seventeen-year-old boys and girls confirms my own observation that when students make connections between the work being studied and something outside the literature, there is a definite difference between the sexes. Girls are likely to draw comparisons *with life or other pieces of literature*; boys are likely to compare *with stories seen on television or in the movies* (Bowman 1992, 81).

There are probably at least two separate factors at work here. Boys are less likely to see links with other pieces of literature because, as I've already said, they have a less rich sense of literary culture: they probably read less than girls and don't have a habit of participating in book talk. Talking about things seen on television or the movies, however, *is* part of boy culture.

The reluctance to draw connections with life, on the other hand, reflects compartmentalization. The book is fiction, and to suggest that it has something to do with my life not only crosses a conceptual boundary, but may also feel like an intrusion. If I (as a boy) value my independence and don't like being exposed, why is the English teacher always being nosey and trying to get me to talk about things in my life? Why can't she just stick to her job of teaching literature? In that reaction, we detect male reticence about expressing emotions (as discussed in Chapter 4), but also confusion about why the teacher is apparently stepping out of the box and mingling storybooks with real life: "I don't think my life is any of the school's business."

I have two suggestions for assisting boys in building connections.

1. Let them in on the reason we look for connections.

One way of looking at this problem is to recognize that students are short on theory. You and I know at least a bit about cognitive processing and reader response theory. When we try to get students to make connections with their lives, it's not because we're nosey. (At least, I hope it isn't.) It's because our professional training tells us that people make sense of things by fitting the new into the familiar and grow by seeing the familiar in light of the new. That's why we push students to mobilize their prior understanding. We know all that, but students haven't had our training. The ones who naturally make a personal investment in their reading and don't mind talking about such things—many girls, in other words—don't have a problem with our strategy, but the boys face what seems like an unjustified personal invasion.

If the problem is a lack of theory, one good, direct remedy is to give them a little theory: let them in on the secret. In *Critical Encounters in High School English*, Deborah Appleman (2000) has written helpfully about teaching a variety of literary theories to older students. Mark Pike (2000), writing about grade 11 boys' antipathy to poetry, describes how he moved from merely *using* a response-based methodology to actually *teaching* that methodology, telling students, for example, about Louise Rosenblatt's (1978) distinction between "efferent" and "aesthetic" readings. With all grades (9 to 12), I draw on the blackboard a book and a giant head (representing the reader) and talk about how there's an interaction (or transaction) between the text and the reader. The text brings certain things to the table and the reader brings certain things, including experiences of life, literature, TV, and movies. I remind them that young children reading a mature piece of literature won't understand as much as an adult, not just because they don't know all the words but because they haven't lived as much. Life experiences include specific events as well as the more general background effects of culture, ethnicity, sex, social status, religion, and so on. Once that much theory has been made explicit, it's not hard for students to see that sifting through the connections made by a reader is an important part of studying how meaning is made, not just an excuse for an invasion of their privacy.

Teaching theory can happen at a pretty basic level. One teacher of weak students told me that her learning disabled boys simply wouldn't make any connections until, in exasperation, she flat-out declared, *"This is what good readers do."* Something clicked, her boys said, "Oh," and they began, according to the teacher, making connections "forever after."

2. Make the fiction live through drama.

I've already talked about the usefulness of drama in giving permission for emotional exploration. Students can use role-playing to deflect the connection with literature onto the life of someone other than themselves. ("Write the response that a soldier might have after reading this story.") Sometimes I have different students prepare a variety of in-role responses, then sit them together to discuss, in their various roles, their different takes on the literature.

Indeed, drama in general is an excellent way of bridging the gap between books and boys. Once a boy gets onto his feet and has to move and talk like a character in a story, perhaps looking his antagonist in the eye, perhaps delivering a eulogy for a friend or a midnight soliloquy that no one (except the audience) can hear, or listening to the pressure of the fictional community being voiced by his classmates, then that story is no longer just words on a page, no longer "just a story." Many girls may find it easy enough to get into stories—imaginatively, empathetically—just by reading those words on the page, but once a boy has a chance to *live* the story, then he can care about it just as passionately, and the fiction becomes real.

Beyond Empathy: Taking the Machine Apart

Awhile ago, our family VCR stopped working. We bought a replacement and I was just about to discard the defunct machine, when, on a hunch, I turned to my son, who was then seven years old, and asked, "Julian, would you like to take the old VCR apart and see what's inside?"

"Would I?!" he replied fervently. "Yes!"

On Saturday, first thing in the morning, we cleared the kitchen table, pulled together an assortment of screwdrivers and pliers, and set to work. With me at his side, he methodically disassembled the unit, carefully piling up the different kinds of components. We had to set the work aside briefly for lunch, but otherwise he worked through the morning and most of the afternoon with unflagging patience. This was no crude act of destruction, but rather a surgical dissection. At each step, he paused to figure out what piece could be loosened next and how to get it out without breaking anything. It turns out that a VCR has scores of pieces that are screwed, snapped, wound, slotted, and otherwise fitted together in more ways than I could have guessed. Once you've figured out each step of the puzzle, a piece comes away cleanly. The only place where glue or solder was used was on the master circuit board, which we left intact, and which Julian keeps as a souvenir to this day.

When he finished in the afternoon, my son heaved a great sigh of satisfaction at a job well done. Obviously, he hadn't learned much about how VCRs work, because the heart of that mystery lies in the circuit board's miniature patterns. But he (and I) learned a lot about the ways in which electronic equipment is assembled: bits of plastic and metal pieced together with myriad ingenious connections.

As I watched and marveled at his absorption, I hoped his teachers would be wise enough to figure out how to tap in to this capacity for sustained effort and learning. Here was a boy willing to put hours of undivided attention into figuring out how a complicated structure was put together, deeply satisfied at the end when he knew that he had achieved a mastery of sorts, that he had worked his way through the network of fittings.

You'll sometimes hear people say that boys prefer quick answers and that they're impatient with the complexities of literary response. It's odd, though, because boys do like complex networks. They like being able to understand computer operating systems. They like figuring out the complexity of interrelated phenomena, like physics, or the Internet, or mazelike computer games. They want to take the machine apart (physically) or get *inside* structures (mentally) and understand how they work.

This is a powerful, masculine inclination toward inquiry and learning. We would be only too grateful if we could harness such concentration in the English classroom. Notice, however, that this style of getting into a subject doesn't have much to do with empathy. It's not about erasing the boundaries between subject and object or "getting lost" in the material being studied. The analytic mind that I'm describing here maintains a critical distance from its material in order to do the job of sorting, classifying, fitting things into compartments, and figuring out the rules that govern whatever system is being analyzed.

This mind-set is a perfectly good way of knowing the world. It's a way of thinking that rings the right bells for a boy who has even the most blinkered set of dominant masculine attitudes. It is a way of thinking that serves him well in his math and science classes.

It is not, however, necessarily what that boy hears when he enters the English classroom. He may instead hear characters from books being talked about as if they were real people, which offends his common sense. He may hear—or think he hears—that he is supposed to feel that he's right inside a fictional character, and that he has been swept into an emotional experience by the literature. If he doesn't have those experiences, well then, there must be something wrong with him. Maybe he's just an insensitive male.

That kind of talk rings the wrong bells.

By now, you may think I am contradicting myself. In the previous section, didn't I say we should find ways to help boys connect with literature, bridge the gap between fiction and reality, and find empathy within themselves? Yes, that's what I said. And now I'm saying that there should be distanced analysis and less talk of empathy and involvement? Yes, that's right.

Does that sound contradictory? Only if you think a person has to be one or the other: either a passionate, connected thinker or a detached analyst, but never both. A cornerstone of my argument in this book is that we all—men and women—can be more than we are, and that we all would be enlarged by thinking in more than one way. I believe that a good teacher reaches out to learners with *two* hands: one hand supporting and encouraging the strengths that are already there, and the other hand pushing the learner to attempt kinds of behavior, learning, and thinking that perhaps do not come naturally. That is why I can say, yes, we want to teach boys how to immerse themselves empathetically in reading, *but empathy isn't everything.* There are other valid ways of making sense of the things we read, and we can honor those ways as well. To do less than this is to shortchange both the boys and the girls, all of whom need to move beyond their present repertoire of reading habits.

Beyond empathy is the critical recognition that literary objects, like VCRs, are constructed by human hands. They are put together purposefully, and figuring out how that has been done is important learning (Mackey 2000, 182). A similar thought appears in an official British document about raising boys' achievement in English:

> *Stories are often studied in order to consider characters, their feelings and relationships; areas which girls tend to find appealing. . . . If narrative were treated less as though it were about real people and more about how meaning is constructed and understood by different readers, then boys may join in more readily. (QCA 1998, 18)*

We can't abandon the study of characters' feelings and relationships: that study is important for the students who find that appealing and perhaps even more important for all the students who don't, because they're the ones who most need to be challenged and stretched to think about such things. Having said that, however, we must recognize that there are also ways of thinking about literature as a construction and looking at its "machinery"—ways of thinking that complement rather than replace empathetic reading.

After all, we're surrounded by a whole culture of constructed images and narratives, including the pitches of political and commercial advertising. We're not going to get far in the world if all we can do is immerse ourselves and "empathize" with all those stories; we have to develop critical and analytical distance as well.

The Media Connection: Constructed Like a Movie

If boys are more likely to make connections with film and television, we can exploit that as a way of making sense of how literature works. There are standard situations and characters that keep recurring throughout our culture, including the popular media. If we want students to understand how cultural objects are put together, we can't be shy about using the narratives that they know and helping them to see how writers choose and use particular pieces of machinery. That's why when I'm inviting students to find connections, I always describe them as "connections with other things that you've read, *or with TV or movies you've seen*," thus giving boys permission to mobilize their own expertise. Students' appreciation of *To Kill a Mockingbird* is enhanced when they realize that Harper Lee is using for her own purposes familiar archetypes such as the spooky house, the mysterious recluse, the virtuous lawyer, the tomboy, the victim of injustice, and the dangerous walk on a dark Halloween night. If you've seen lots of movies, you're well on your way to understanding the construction of that novel.

Here's a practical example of how popular culture can be used to help with reading. A group of students was making a presentation in which they discussed the brutal killing of the sow in *Lord of the Flies*. They made several salient observations about Golding's imagery, but they were stumped by the butterflies that flutter through the scene at one point. One boy said, "They're pretty and they're innocent. They don't really belong, so I don't know." He continued, appealing to the class, "Does anyone have any idea what the author means by this?"

This drew a blank. From the back of the room, I suggested, "Maybe rather than asking what the author *means*, we could ask what he's *doing* and what effect that has. He's putting something delicate and beautiful into a disturbing and violent scene. Have you ever seen any films that do something like that?"

I wanted to get off the question of what it *means*, because that can be a roadblock, raising the shibboleth of "hidden meanings" and all the instinctive insecurities about understanding books. ("I never know what these deep things mean.") It can be more useful to think instead of the text as *doing* something, like a film. It was a gamble, but it paid off because there were instantly lots of hands up—lots of boys' hands especially. They had plenty of examples of film horror being underscored with sweet music or pretty images. Actually, I didn't recognize most of their examples, but they all seemed to know these movies, and they were able to talk easily about the chilling impact of such irony. The aesthetics of Golding's imagery made perfect sense when approached through a parallel with film.

When studying a book like *Lord of the Flies*, mobilizing knowledge of "shipwrecked and stranded" movies can help students see the overall shape of Golding's narrative. A couple of decades ago, the most obvious TV parallel would have been *Gilligan's Island*. Recently, students are more likely to think of the *Survivor* series, and its scheming subplots and rivalries make for fruitful comparisons with *Lord of the Flies*. When one of the contestants in *The Australian Outback* version of *Survivor* became obsessed with killing a pig and even painted his face with blood, there was an eerie link between fiction and "reality TV." Students generally realize that a show like *Survivor* is heavily edited to construct a dramatic story line, and that same understanding can be brought to bear on the reading of literature, because Golding too, like any author or any movie director, selects and shapes his material.

My next example demonstrates how students can learn how selecting and shaping are part of text construction. In effect, this approach validates the male instinct to insist that books and reality are separate and should not be confused.

Seeing the Difference Between Text and Reality

For several years, I've had students read a short essay, originally published as a newspaper article, about a homeless woman living on the streets of Toronto, all her possessions in a beat-up suitcase (McLaren 1981). (You could easily find a similar work relevant to your own locale: any article that shows us life "as it really is.") The piece clearly makes a bid for our feelings. The journalist interviews the "suitcase lady," describes her pathetic appearance, and lets us hear her words. The intention of the article is unmistakable: we are supposed to feel a mix of sympathy, pity, and empathy, as well as respect for the woman's endurance. Like much nonfiction and realistic fiction, the piece invites us to believe that the boundaries between reader and subject have evaporated, and that we are right there in the coffee shop, face-to-face with this woman.

The article does its job well and shakes the complacency of some students. We talk about how different people might have different reactions to this piece and how our reactions say something about our own situations in life. Inevitably, a student mentions the impression of being "right there" or of being made to see the "reality" of street life. At that point, I remind them that that is an illusion. In fact, they *aren't* "right there":

they're sitting in a comfortable classroom looking at a newspaper story reprinted in a textbook. On the blackboard, I quickly sketch the homeless woman and, at a distance, a representative student, textbook in hand. When I ask what has to be added to the picture, the answer, of course, is the interviewer, who acts as an intermediary.

I point out that the interviewer is a trained writer constructing a version of reality: we should expect that she would use the techniques she has learned in journalism school to shape the picture she wants us to see. At that point, students form pairs and I assign each pair a few short paragraphs from the text, asking them quickly to find evidence of a writer "doing the kinds of things that writers do." This includes using figures of speech, clever wording, selecting just the right detail, using sentence structure to highlight a point, and so on. (The age and prior learning of your students will determine how much explanation that instruction requires.)

Within a few minutes, students all over the room have found evidence of a writer at work. There are loaded metaphors, details chosen for their poignancy, a subtle suggestion that the old woman is a version of Cinderella in the ashes, waiting to be discovered by a prince, and more. As they recognize this constructedness, students also see that the whole piece has been carefully crafted to shape their response and that its realism is a clever illusion.

One year, a student pointed out something that I had missed. The editor of our anthology tells us that the author spent "several nights" with the suitcase lady. The student observed that over several nights there must have been a lot more things said than we eventually read in the short article. What sort of material was the writer choosing to exclude? Obviously, the writer decided on an angle for the story—a kind of romanticizing of the derelict woman—and would leave out anything that didn't fit that story line. It wasn't hard for us to imagine what kinds of things wouldn't make the final cut, including sordid details and alternative voices that might have had something else to say about this woman. We even played at composing what those voices might say.

It's important for students to realize that this isn't a complaint about the author. Teenagers—perhaps boys especially—can be triumphantly smug when they think they've found someone hiding something: "She's trying to cover something up!" They need to understand that no writer (or photographer or filmmaker) could ever show us *all* reality. Telling a story, even a story about what you did on the weekend, *always* means selecting certain details that fit together meaningfully and leaving out piles of other details that someone else might have used to construct an entirely different representation. That's not an accusation that someone is deceiving us: it's just recognition of what it's like to use the tools of representation. It's a recognition that allows us to be critically aware because we understand how the machinery works.

Once, after we had been doing work like this in a senior course, a girl lingered after class and said thoughtfully, "You know, it's kind of funny. It seems that all these years teachers have been telling us that we should try to get *into* the book and just let the author work on us. Now in this class we seem to be backing off, questioning what the writers are doing and also what they aren't doing. It's different."

It is different, and in the end, I told this student, we hope that we can still get into books, but it will be a getting in that's a bit more educated and aware, not a blind surrender.

It's good for all of our students to develop critical awareness and an understanding of the machinery of culture, but it can be especially important for boys because it may validate a way of learning that feels right to them. It's good for them to see that English isn't just about pretending that fictions are real and telling everyone about your feelings. It isn't about guessing hidden meanings and copying down what someone else said was the theme of the book. All that is too easily dismissed as not being real or important work. If that's all English and reading amount to, then some of those boys are right: they probably do have better things to do.

Instead, we can deliver the message that English demands sharp analytic minds that understand the difference between fiction and reality, between a romantic myth and the harsh reality of a homeless woman. We can prove that English is about understanding how we make sense of our world, our culture, and ourselves. It's about finding out how the machinery of meaning making works.

Those are important things for a school subject to be about. Who could claim to have better things to do?

7 *Classroom Visit*

Grade 10, Academic

Pam Richardson's grade 10 class has twenty one girls and only nine boys. The course is labeled "academic," which means students have enrolled in it because they and their parents see university in their future. Some will, no doubt, have to reassess that plan. Before I visit, Pam tells me that there are a lot of forceful young women in the room. In terms of their social and emotional maturity, several of the girls in the class are, in Pam's words, "fifteen years old, going on twenty-five."

At the time of my visit, students are beginning group work on the novel *Lord of the Flies*. They have already taken a quiz to prove that they have read the book, and Pam has used those scores to create groupings: each group has students with similar scores. Pam figures it isn't fair, in group work, for the best students to have to bear the burden of others who haven't been as conscientious in reading the book. That sorting has created a bottom-rung group of five boys. In other words, of the nine boys in the class, more than half either have not completed the assigned reading or have read it too poorly to do well on the test, and they will now work with one another on this project. The other four boys, with better scores, are scattered through the rest of the class, one per group.

I'm looking forward to seeing how this arrangement works. We know that if left to their own preferences, students often choose same-sex groups but may not mind if a teacher assigns them to mixed groups. There is evidence that, by grade 8, both boys and girls respond well to either same-sex or mixed-sex groups, as long as the numbers are balanced. Generally, neither sex likes to be in the minority—the single boy in a group of girls or vice versa (Grima 1999). Of course, when boys are outnumbered two to one, as they are in Pam's class, balanced groupings are hard to create, especially when an achievement measure herds five of them into an all-boy group.

They begin with a follow-up discussion of the previous day's activity, which had been a "survivor" task. They were asked to imagine being

101

stranded on an uninhabited island. Each group had a list of possible supplies and had to reach a consensus about which items to keep. Today's
focus will be on group processes: they will reflect on how their group
handled yesterday's consensus-building task. (This issue is relevant to the
challenge of group decision making faced by the boys in Golding's novel.)

I choose a few groups for closer observation. First, I move to the five
boys in the low-level group. Being placed in this group probably means
they don't know much about the book, but that's not a hindrance yet,
because yesterday's survivor activity didn't require any knowledge of the
text. They seem to have enjoyed yesterday's work. That's not surprising.
There was a concrete problem to be solved—which supplies to keep—
and lots of commentators have noted that boys like to be cast in the role
of problem solvers (Tannen 1990, 52; Gurian 1998, 35; Kindlon and
Thompson 1999, 247). One of the things Pam has suggested for the
groups today is that they should ask themselves whether they are happy
with the decisions reached yesterday. This boy group latches on to that
one suggestion and uses it as an excuse to replay yesterday's work, which
for this group seems to have been an enjoyable battle. Each boy has a
different idea of what supplies to keep on their island and it appears that
they fought fiercely yesterday to champion their own lists. I'm not sure
they have reached anything that I would call a consensus: I suspect
they've verbally hammered each other into submission, and they're treat-
ing today's "reflection" as if the lid has been lifted on yesterday's squabble
and they can dive in again.

It's all a great pleasure for them. These boys are having fun. They are
laughing, insulting each other, all the while staying focused on the survivor question. The task was intended by the teacher as a collaborative
exercise, but this group has redefined it as an occasion for combat, a
classic example of male competitiveness. From early childhood, girls can
be seen at more collaborative play while boys gravitate to competition
(Maccoby 1998, 39). What I'm seeing in this grade 10 group is a direct
extension of the way these same boys might have reveled in rough-and-
tumble play-fights when they were in grade 5. It might seem that this
means boys are more individualistic or separated, while girls are more
connected or collective, but this kind of play does in fact tie boys together.
They genuinely like each other better because they can interact this way.
They are excited by the challenge. There is physiological evidence that
boys are pleasurably aroused by threats and challenges in a way that girls
aren't (Maccoby 1998, 115–16). This could be a reason for younger boys
often preferring male playmates, who understand this pleasure, as opposed to girls, who may be baffled by what they see as the immaturity
of boys' play. ("All they ever do is fight!")

By the time they reach adolescence, males are reaching a point where this drive needs to be harnessed productively. Although these boys are enjoying English class today, I can't see that they're getting very far in terms of Pam's goals for them. Their squabbling is repetitive, and I grow bored and move away to another group.

Judged by their quiz scores, the next group has middling achievement. Just by watching eye contact, it becomes clear that Adam, the single boy in the group, has emerged as the leader. Almost all remarks made by the three girls are addressed to him. Far from feeling oppressed by his minority status, he revels in his role. He is popular, genial, chatty, and seems to be setting the agenda—at least the overt agenda. There may also be some covert agendas at work here: Pam tells me that Adam is an ex-boyfriend of one of the girls in this group and it is widely known that other girls in the room have their eyes on him. As always when working with adolescents, we have to remember that classroom talk and behavior may be strategic moves in a complicated game of peer relationships.

After a few more minutes of group talk, Pam hands out a page with definitions of different group roles: dominating, withdrawing, focusing, listening, distracting, encouraging, and so on. Students are given a few minutes to complete a self-assessment questionnaire on their own styles in the present group. ("Did you feel you were listened to?" "Who emerged as a leader?" "Which style best describes you?") They are then asked to share the results with their group members.

Adam has identified himself, correctly, I think, as a dominator, and the girls agree. Although the definition handed out makes this seem (to me) like a negative role—a dominator "interrupts," "asserts authority," and "monopolizes discussion"—Adam is beaming with pleasure. He is delighted with the label. Of course, these are all conventional masculine qualities: men are supposed to be dominant and assertive. Being able to interrupt and monopolize conversations may be confirmation of his manly status. Adam willingly accepts the mantle of the dominator, and the three girls willingly agree with him. There's a joking and teasing quality to all of this, as if they all recognize the negative connotations but wouldn't consider trying to change anything. ("Yeah, it's true," Adam says disarmingly while laughing, "I'm always doing that.") As I watch, I'm well aware of the complaint that girls suffer in schools because boys take over discussions, and it's a bit worrying to see the traditional role of dominance falling so easily on the sole male, and to see the apparently cheerful compliance by the circle of girls.

I eavesdrop back on the first group of boys for a moment, long enough to pick up that they all seem to have described themselves as dominators. I'm not surprised.

In the meantime, I've also been watching another group, where a different version of masculinity is playing itself out. Steve, also the lone boy in a group with four girls, seems out of his element. The girls in his group are forceful in the initial discussion, often picking up the previous speaker's words in mid-sentence and eagerly carrying on the thought. This is not so much a pattern of interruption as a matter of picking up the action, like basketball players who work well at passing the ball or jazz musicians who smoothly improvise transitions between soloists.

"I mean, we were right to say our top priority was being rescued. So you've got to see that the boat . . ."

". . . the boat has to stay. It's the one thing . . ."

". . . it's your whole reason . . ."

". . . your reason, yeah. It's your hope . . ."

Linguists identify this overlapping style, with participants collectively weaving a fabric of conversation, as a common characteristic of women's talk, while men are often more likely to adhere to one-at-a-time turn taking, unless they're openly trying to defeat the other person's ideas (Coates 1997, 126). It's not that men and women can't ever use the style associated with the other sex, but most of us do have preferred styles. Faced with a group that has adopted an incompatible pattern of talk, individuals react in different ways. Some shift registers easily and think nothing of it. Others may try to wrestle control of the discussion and shape it into their own style. Others force themselves to adapt but feel awkwardly self-conscious. Still others retreat into silence.

Steve takes the latter approach. He keeps his head down and appears to be listening, but says nothing. I don't think the girls are deliberately excluding him. It's just that they have slipped into a conversational pattern that feels natural to them. If we see this as a kind of game, then it's a game that Steve can't play very well: he's never able to grab the ball.

When it comes time for them to fill out the self-assessment questionnaire, I notice that Steve curls up the edge of his paper, blocking the girls from seeing his answers, although, as far as I can make out, they have no interest in what he writes. It seems that for Steve, his experience of this group is a private and delicate matter: he's taking the questionnaire seriously and has some anxiety about self-revelation. While the students write, I get up and stroll around the room, casually glancing at student work. Steve doesn't block me from seeing his page, and I note that he has circled "listener" as the label for his role in the group. That role is described as "not giving too many of your own ideas" and "observing the participation of others."

The sharing time begins and three of the girls excitedly and freely compare their questionnaires. The fourth girl, Wendy, who sits immediately beside Steve, turns to him and initiates a very quiet conversation.

Smiling nervously, Steve lets her see his questionnaire and they seem to be talking agreeably about what each has written. I can't hear what they're saying, but my reading of the situation is that, while the other three girls are cheerfully wrapped up in their own triad, Wendy, who had previously been an active part of the main conversation, has had the sensitivity to realize that Steve was being left out. Tactfully, she has found a low-key way of opening up talk about this self-assessment. Steve seems shyly pleased with the conversation. It probably helps that Wendy happens to be sitting beside him, allowing them to be shoulder-to-shoulder rather than face-to-face, which would feel more confrontational. I imagine that if the girl sitting *across* the table had said loudly, "So, Steve, show us what you've written," Steve would have shrunk.

Talking about yourself and how you communicate with other people can be risky. It is a kind of emotion talk and we know it is uncomfortable for some men and boys—apparently not for Adam in the group discussed previously, but probably for Steve. The interesting point is that, in the end, I don't think Steve minded delving into this topic *per se*. What was crucial was the *approach*. If it meant getting himself up to the group's overall speed and joining the girls' conversation, it probably wasn't going to happen, but a quiet side-by-side chat with a tactful partner worked well.

In the next chapter, I'll take a more detailed look at how we can help students develop their awareness of what's going on in situations like this and develop their own capacity for oral communication, but we can see this taking shape in the work Pam is doing here, getting kids to pay attention to the way they interact with others. After the groups have had a few minutes to discuss their questionnaires, she brings the whole class together for a wrap-up session. She asks if anyone has ever had the experience, successful or not, of trying to encourage someone to be more productive in a group. A number of girls are happy to offer anecdotes. The girls' stories are all about *boys* who weren't being constructive or boys who insisted that they ought to do all the technical work (with video editing equipment, for example). The boys in the class listen to this attentively, without comment. Pam talks a little about the difficulty of dealing with dominators and half-jokingly says, "There are a lot of dominant personalities in this class." I believe her, and in this class I see that dominance comes in a variety of forms.

The groups in Pam's class now go on to work up presentations based on topics related to *Lord of the Flies*. I come back a week later to see their presentations. They are based on traditional ideas like theme, character, and setting. Each group has half an hour to teach its topic to the class. Their lessons will include handouts and some element of dramatization.

The first presentation is by the group that includes Steve, the boy who had had difficulty entering the girls' conversation on my first visit. They have decided to explore Ralph's character by dramatizing an imaginary session in which Ralph, played by Steve, undergoes therapy with a group of counselors, played by the girls, after his return from the island. The girls gather their chairs into a tight semicircle at the front of the room; they seem huddled together protectively. Steve, on the other hand, has a sharp sense of audience and angles his chair out from the "therapy circle" so that we in the rest of the room can see his face. He proceeds to enact a vigorous characterization of Ralph, with a strong sense of the distress that Ralph might feel after what happened on the island.

What a different boy I am seeing today! Steve is large and entertaining, confident enough to mix improvisation with his prepared performance. It is as if Steve and the girls each have different, complementary faces that come out on different occasions: in the small group, the girls were dynamic while Steve was shy and marginalized; in the public performance before the class, the girls are nearly immobilized but Steve comes alive.

I don't want to overgeneralize from this one example. I've certainly seen girls who, given the chance, transform themselves into performers, and I've seen plenty of boys who are mortified by the thought of speaking to a large group. Still, I can't help recalling Deborah Tannen's distinction between "public" and "private" speaking and her observation that many women prefer small groups that can be approached as a venue for private speaking and building personal bonds. Men, on the other hand, says Tannen, seek status and attention and, in order to gain that attention, are often more comfortable with larger audiences and "verbal performance such as story-telling, joking, or imparting information" (1990, 77). Thus we have the parallel phenomena of the man who gives entertaining speeches but can't handle small talk, and the woman who chats easily with three or four friends but freezes at the thought of speaking before a larger assembly. This simple formula seems to fit this group, doesn't it?

But that isn't the end of their presentation. After a few more short dramatizations, they move on to a character overview. Using an overhead projector, the group shows us a point-form summary, and they take turns presenting the main characters.

Now I see yet another side to Steve. This segment requires him to stand and explain the essential characteristics of Ralph. To use Tannen's terminology, it's still public talk, this time "imparting information," which one might expect him to do well. Suddenly, however, Steve dries up. All he can do now is read the few words from the overhead: one- or two-word descriptors of Ralph, followed by a terse mention of evidence from the novel.

> *He's a born leader. That's because he put Jack in charge of the choir. And he's open, because he talked about being afraid of the beast. And he has survival skills. He builds the hut.*

It's a recitation of separate traits, label and proof, a mechanical checklist, coming from a boy who had, a few minutes earlier, made this same character live before our eyes.

It is in stark contrast to what follows when Wendy steps up to cover the character of Piggy. Here's one example of how she pulls threads out of a moment in the novel:

> *When Piggy loses his glasses we hear him whining, which is what he has always done. And he's outraged that they would do this. But also there's panic now. He's panicking because he has lost an important connection with the world. He's really pathetic now, begging Ralph to stay within reach.*

Wendy takes this one incident and considers the different facets and shadings of emotion, fleshing out our understanding. The other girls in the group follow, and each similarly delivers something that we would probably recognize as being more like literary analysis than the bare bones of Steve's report.

Steve's understanding can be communicated beautifully when he is allowed to dramatize, and we need to make sure that he gets the chance to demonstrate that to us and to himself. We also need to make sure that we show him how those other sorts of talk work. For example, we might notice that Wendy is working *inductively*—starting with the concrete event and seeing where that leads, which takes her to the abstractions of Piggy's emotional state. Steve, on the other hand, may be working more *deductively*. When Steve attempts "literature talk," he seems to be controlled first by his list of abstractions ("leadership," "openness," "survivor skills"), to which he attaches the obligatory evidence.

Of course, not all boys come alive with drama. The next presentation is by the group that has Adam, the boy who was the proud dominator of his group of girls. They too offer a dramatized therapy encounter. This time it's group therapy, with Jack and Ralph at the same session, complete with dramatized flashbacks. It's a fairly hokey re-creation of violent moments in the novel, but what interests me is the muted role played by Adam. When I had seen him talking with his group on the previous occasion, he seemed confident and in charge. In today's role-playing he is a bit lost, looking nervously to the girls for leadership, perhaps afraid to go too far and embarrass himself. I wonder if there's a general principle here: Steve, who is muted in small-group conversation, comes alive with drama, while Adam, who is forceful with his group, falters on stage.

I've been waiting with particular interest to see what happens with the all-boy group, the group that had the handicap of being a collection of the weakest students on the initial quiz. I arrive the next day only to find that there has been a hitch in the plans and the boys are pleading with Pam for an extension of their due date. One boy was absent yesterday, and someone else the day before. Attendance, of course, is often a problem with lower achievers. Strictly speaking, this shouldn't make any difference today, because they have been seeing presentations for the past two days, not using class time for their own preparations. Their work was all supposed to have been prepared by the end of the previous week, but they confess that they aren't ready yet.

Pam is frustrated and annoyed but not surprised. The rough-and-tumble style that I saw earlier in this group has prevented them from cooperating successfully. Masculine competitiveness *can* be harnessed into successful teamwork *if* there's a strong sense of the guys having to work together to compete against other teams. However, in this assignment, there hasn't been a strong sense of competition between groups. In the absence of an external rival to focus their combat, they have turned their instincts inward and spent the last week bickering with one another. I suppose we could make everything in the classroom always a contest, and some boys would probably like that, but lots of girls (and lots of boys) wouldn't, especially when they turn out to be the contest losers. The more sound response, I think, is to offer these boys some pretty direct instruction, including role modeling, in cooperative behavior. (That's where we're going in the next chapter.)

Pam reluctantly grants them an extension, and I return the next day, finally to see the boy group. Their topic is "Title, Theme, and Moral" in *Lord of the Flies*.

I would love to have a surprise ending to this chapter. Wouldn't it be ironic if this apparently doomed group turned out to have the best presentation in the class? If they were to create a moving drama that caught the essence of the male trauma at the heart of this novel?

It doesn't happen that way.

Their idea of dramatization is to read out a few passages from the book, one boy reading the narration and others the dialogue, not always the right lines, not even always on the right page. There is a small moment of excitement when they enact the killing of Simon. They have recruited a volunteer from the class to play the victim and enjoy poking him with sticks as they circle and chant, "Kill the pig! Spill his blood!" After each mini-enactment, they offer commentary like, "That was a real highlight in the book," or they laboriously read out packaged comments that have the ring of Cliff's Notes or something found on a website. At one point, they realize their notes are out of order; we wait for them to shuffle their papers, whispering recriminations at one another. Then they need to refer to a page in the novel but discover that there are two different editions of the text and their page numbers don't match. Painfully, we wait for them to thumb through their books, looking for the right page. We know that when they find it, it won't have been worth the wait.

I don't need to prolong this story of their humiliation. It is a poor job. They know they don't really have anything to say, and the best they're hoping for is to disguise the full extent of what they don't have to offer. They haven't learned much, and the class doesn't learn much from them. I could make it sound funny, but in truth it was sad. They have wasted not just the half hour of today's class but all the time they spent supposedly preparing this work.

What haunts me is the thought that these five boys were doomed from the start, from the moment they were placed in a group with other boys who had also done poorly on the quiz. I don't mean to condemn Pam's decision to group the class this way. She acted conscientiously and in good faith, based on her judgment that planting any of those boys in other groups would have unfairly burdened those groups with a member who wouldn't be able to contribute fully. Instead, she gave those weaker students a chance to show what they could do when they worked with others at comparable levels of achievement. Plenty of official streaming in schools is based on exactly those principles, so we can hardly blame Pam for doing something that is consistent with institutional policy and also probably matches what many of us have done in one way or other, at one time or other.

Still, as we see the outcome of this project, we have to wonder whether this was the best course of action. The answer isn't obvious. If we could turn back the clock and group that class differently, perhaps randomly, some of those boys might have been pulled up to the level of their peers.

Or they might have wasted everyone's time even more, annoyed their groups, and lowered the quality of work all around the room.

I know my instinct is usually not to group by ability, but I also know that that second scenario is entirely possible. At least, as I say, we have to wonder how things might have been made to turn out differently.

I said the boys were doomed from the moment they were put into this group, but really, Pam wasn't the executor of their fates. Those boys made their own decisions about reading the book and about handling the group work. Others might say that if there was any doom, it happened long before Pam's assignment. The chain of circumstance that made them the boys that they are stretches far beyond the classroom walls, back to the cradle and further still.

That chain is real, and it's our job not to accept the doom, but to look to the future and to see with our students how they can get footholds on the paths that lead on most productively from where they are now.

8 *They Just Don't Listen!*

Speaking and Listening

It's hard to ignore gender differences when you watch kids talking together in classrooms. When teachers complain that discussions, whether in small or large groups, are difficult to manage, it often turns out that the most conspicuous difficulties are created by boys. You don't have to be prejudiced to know that certain laments are frequently heard in the staff room, and that those laments have reason.

"The boys in that class are such yahoos! There's a gang of them that's loud and obnoxious from the minute they walk into the room. They never settle down, and I spend half my time trying to control them."

"They have an opinion about everything, even if they don't know what they're talking about. They'll argue anything, just to hear themselves. Most of the girls won't speak at all, because they know some boy will find a stupid way of arguing them down."

Or, "The boys just sit there. I can't get them to say anything. Every day, the whole discussion is carried by the girls."

Or, "When I put them into groups, the boys just take over. They won't take seriously anything a girl says."

"Those boys are so immature. Whenever there's any chance of talking about something important, one of them finds a way to break it up. The girls roll their eyes."

"They're just plain rude."

When we find ourselves thinking these thoughts, we should remind ourselves that there are always varieties of masculinities at work. There may be a gang of yahoos, but that shouldn't blind us to the other boys in the class or to differences between the yahoos themselves. There are variations within the negative versions of masculinity: some boys are belligerent and aggressive, while others are passive and withdrawn. We should notice the quiet and thoughtful boys on the sidelines. Also, there are different layers within any individual boy. No one is all yahoo, all the time: there was a wide range of male behavior seen in Pam Richardson's grade 10 class, as I described it in Chapter 7. We should beware our tendency to pay most attention to the loudest individuals, who sometimes control our impression of what boys are.

Teaching communication skills is our job. Learning English (like learning math, science, or history) means learning how to read and write like an English student and also how to speak and listen like an English student—ultimately, how to communicate like a fully functioning human being. Some would write off communication styles as innate personality rather than learned skills, but if we say that, we abandon the chance to make an important difference in students' lives.

There is evidence that at least some of the differences between male and female styles of talk have more to do with the contexts in which men and women commonly find themselves than with any innate sex-specific characteristics. In other words, it's not that boys *can't* listen empathetically or speak cooperatively; it's just that many of the activities in which they find themselves don't induce those types of communication. Men who do find themselves engaging in "women's" activities may use language in much the same way as women would (Corson 2001, 155). Therapists have to learn to speak in connected, supportive, empathetic ways—traditionally female strengths—and one study has found that while inexperienced male therapists can't do that as well as women, that difference disappears over time and with practice. Similarly, women who take assertiveness training learn to turn off tentative and self-deprecating speech mannerisms (Tannen 1990, 121–22). Linguist Deborah Cameron describes a group gossiping, offering understanding to each other, and supportively picking up the threads of each other's unfinished sentences to weave a shared conversation. Those qualities are all usually ascribed to women, but the group in question was in fact a number of male college students watching a basketball game on television (1997, 55–58).

Cultural expectations may push us all to talk in predictable and habitual ways, but these occasional glimpses of variations tell us that boys and girls don't actually come from different planets. They have heard other ways of talking in their lives and, in the right circumstances and with the right support, they can join those other forms of discourse. That doesn't mean it's easy for anyone to change conversational patterns. It's not enough just to say, "I know you can interact differently because I know how you talk with me after class, so go ahead and talk like that right now in front of the class." Contexts can be powerful constraints: it's a hard job to change behaviors that have become habitual within particular contexts. At least the classroom is the one context that we have a chance of influencing. We need to make it a place where boys can "do so-called 'feminine' talk without threatening their constitution as men" (Cameron 1997, 60).

If language differences arise out of specific contexts, then when we encourage boys to attempt different forms of communication in the English classroom, we aren't trying to *rewire* boys' brains or *emasculate* them so that they "talk like girls." Both boys and girls have a large stock of *potential* forms of conversation, even if much of that stock wastes away unused. Our job is to find ways to develop linguistic flexibility in all kids. Both sexes need to know that they have access to a variety of language tools, some of them better suited for specific moments and purposes.

Segregation Versus Integration

Some would argue that one way of handling the different communication and learning styles of boys and girls is to put them into separate schools, or, at least, separate classrooms. As the discussion of boys' education gains momentum in the next few years, the merits of single-sex education are sure to be debated. Such debate is likely to have political overtones in the United States, where legislation guarantees nondiscrimination in publicly funded education, and where the painful history of racially segregated schooling makes people wary of "separate but equal" education.

I confess I cannot speak with the authority of experience: I have never taught in a single-sex classroom. I'm sure some of you have, and when I listen to teachers who work in private boys' or girls' schools, they are almost always positive about single-sex education. (Of course, teachers in coeducational settings are also usually positive about their own systems.)

Writers of popular works about boys are sometimes intrigued by the idea of a boys-only education. For example, both Michael Gurian, in *A Fine Young Man* (1998, 198–205), and William Pollack, in *Real Boys* (1998, 259), express interest in the achievement and self-esteem that might grow in a classroom where there is no distraction from the other sex and where education might be tailored to boys' learning styles. I've already suggested that boys are a varied enough group that there is unlikely to be any one system that's right for all of them. I'm also cautious about the idea that getting rid of the opposite sex eliminates distractions. Boys' posturing is at least as much for the audience of male peers as it is for girls, and men in the absence of women still struggle to work out a hierarchy among themselves. In fact, for many boys, frank discussion may be *easier* with girls than with other boys (Maccoby 1998, 200–201; Harter, Waters, and Whitesell 1997, 164). Removing girls from the room doesn't automatically turn schoolboys into a motivated learning community.

In any case, solid evidence of any such benefit hasn't yet been established. There has been very little examination of single-sex education for boys. There is early evidence of academic benefits for some girls (Maccoby 1998, 309), although the apparently higher achievement in segregated schools often turns out to be an effect of selection processes that send the most capable or privileged students to private, all-girls programs (Arnot et al. 1998, 46). At the moment, it is too early for anyone to claim that research proves anything about boys-only education.

In my chapters on writing and reading and again in this chapter, I generally take the line that boys and girls have lots to learn from each other. If we agree that polarization into "us and them" male/female categories is detrimental, it seems most likely that an integrated education has the best chance of breaking down boundaries. Racially segregated schools did nothing to advance interracial understanding; any form of segregation is likely to turn the "other" into an object of stereotyping. Integrated education has the potential to encourage boys and girls to work, learn, and think together, rather than limiting their contact to specialized occasions like dating (Matthews 1998, 181).

The Classroom Context: More Than Just Throwing Them Together

In the foreseeable future, most young people in North America are likely to be taught in mixed-sex schools. I could paint an idealistic picture of the mutual learning that ought to take place between the sexes: boys learning from girls to be more sensitive and cooperative listeners, girls learning from boys to be more assertive and competitive defenders of their own ideas. However, if you've worked in schools, you know the reality is often closer to the complaints I quoted at the beginning of this chapter. Just throwing kids together in the same room doesn't guarantee learning. That's where teachers come in: we have to be deliberate about shaping the classroom context so that the best is brought out in all our students. There are several things we can do to achieve this.

From an early age, children left to form their own groupings choose playmates or work partners of the same sex. This remains true even through the high school years, when there is new interest in the other sex (Maccoby 1998, 192). As a result, allowing students to choose their own groups typically results in de facto streaming: girl groups and boy groups. Because boys will, on average, have lower achievement levels, there will often be one or more groups of low-achieving boys. Under these conditions, there's a pretty good chance that predictable, stereotyped behaviors will be reinforced.

Of course, students sometimes need the comfort of working alongside their friends. My compromise is to allow them to choose their own home seats in the classroom. This means that they are likely sitting with friends, and, yes, it means that there are often clear gender territories in the room. However, when group work is assigned (which is frequently), I almost always create random groupings by numbering students and sending them off to meet with a new mix of kids. I'm open with them about my purposes for this: "I know you like to work sometimes with your friends, but I also want you to see what can be learned by working with lots of other people." I have observed in secondary students what Barrie Thorne noticed in her study of grade 4 and 5 students: kids are often relieved to have a teacher take responsibility and intervene in this way (1993, 163).

Once we've mixed the students together, our job has only begun. As with writing and reading, we have to be explicit about what it takes to work successfully as a team; it is voodoo pedagogy to dump kids into group work and just *expect* the experience to work well. Teachers in England have been officially advised:

> *If boys prefer to be active and doing, then their ability to listen and respond may be underdeveloped. In group discussion and interaction, . . . it is important that they are taught skills which will enable them to participate in groups in different ways, taking a variety of roles. . . . Being aware of different levels of formality and of how to support others in group discussion are skills which boys may take longer to learn than girls and teaching should take this into account. (QCA 1998, 16–17)*

In particular, we have to recognize the possibility that forceful boys might dominate mixed groups, drowning out what might have been the more careful and thoughtful contributions of girls and quieter boys (Head 1999, 67). Partly, this is a disciplinary, classroom management function of any teacher: we always have to work at establishing a tone of respectful cooperation. It is also something that can be taught directly, as we will see in this chapter.

A Student Investigation of Group Communication

Students need monitoring, feedback, and teaching in order to make the best of group work. Fortunately, we can share with *them* the job of monitoring and delivering feedback and we can get *them* to develop the explicit guidelines. As with reading, the question is "Who should be doing the most thinking about communication styles?" and the answer is "The students." This is sound pedagogy for all students because it passes the bulk of the inquiry and learning into students' hands, but it's also good "boy pedagogy" because it challenges boys to become experts who understand how something works and can give advice to others. In *Raising Cain*,

Dan Kindlon and Michael Thompson make that one of their key recommendations for dealing with boys: they love to be consulted, so "use them as consultants and problem solvers" (1999, 247).

The following set of activities can be attached to any group work that students might normally be doing in class. The class is divided into groups with four, five, or six students per group. They are given a group task relevant to whatever material is being studied at that time. One student in each group is withdrawn and given a "special assignment" as an observer. This observer will not participate in the group's main task; instead, each observer pulls his or her chair back a little from the group and takes notes on the group's communication patterns, using the following guidelines, which are printed on a page for each observer. Each observation task requires only about three minutes. The teacher acts as timekeeper: after three minutes on task 1, the teacher interrupts the groups and asks observers to report to their groups what they were seeing. After a minute or two of that feedback, the teacher tells the groups to continue their work, and the observers to move on to task 2. Again, after a few minutes, work stops so groups can hear the observers' reports, and so on.

See Figure 8.1 for the printed instructions given to observers.

Students are always interested in hearing these reports. It's as if they are seeing themselves in a new kind of mirror, and they immediately begin to shift their manner of speaking and listening. After the first results are reported, everyone suddenly becomes much more self-aware and tries to do a better job of the features discussed by the observer, who has, of course, by then moved on to a new observation task. Most students end up with much sharper awareness of the kinds of things that go on in groups, and that awareness is the first step toward gaining conscious control of their own speaking and listening habits.

This exercise can be repeated on several occasions, perhaps substituting other questions or rearranging the order of tasks. After several sessions like this, it is time for students to become more systematic about their new understanding. I tell them that there are many things a person can do to help make a group work better, as well as many damaging things. I ask them to list as many of these helpful and unhelpful functions as possible. Certain common roles are widely recognized—the distracted ones, the worriers, the synthesizers, the enthusiasts, and so on—and they are well on their way toward constructing their own anatomy of group roles.

The study can take several directions at that point. The general aim is to give students a chance to consolidate the new communications expertise that they have been developing. They could prepare a manual or a workshop demonstrating good group techniques. You might also have each group prepare a scenario demonstrating a particularly difficult group

During each of these tasks, try not to give away exactly what you are watching. (You'll get truer results that way.)

Work on only one task at a time. Start with #1; I'll tell you when to move on to the next one.

After each task, you will report your results to the group and discuss the significance of your findings.

1. Who seems to be emerging as an early leader in this group? How do you know? Jot down observations about that person's leadership signals: words, tone of voice, body language, and positioning. (There may, of course, be more than one person moving into this role. Keep your eyes open!)

2. In a column, list the names of the group members; under the last name, write "nobody." Inside your head, count off ten-second intervals. Every time you get to "ten," put a check beside the name of the person who is talking *at that instant,* or beside "nobody" if there is silence.

3. Select one group member to observe. Make detailed notes on his or her communication in the group. *Remember: 95 percent of communication may be nonverbal:* watch for body language, posture, tone of voice, and so on. Watch for how that person's communication is affected by others.

4. Using a whole sheet of paper, write down the names of the group members in a way that matches how they are positioned around the group. Every time someone speaks, draw an arrow from his or her name to the name of the person he or she seems to be talking to. *(Watch for eye contact.)* There may be more than one arrow for one comment. When someone really seems to be talking to everyone, circle his or her name. (This won't happen often.) For example:

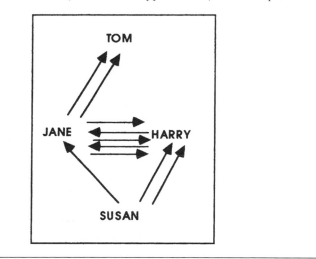

Figure 8.1 Communication patterns

member. After the rest of the class has seen the scenario, the class goes to work problem solving, trying to figure out the best ways of handling the fictitious case.

If you put some time into this kind of work, you can expect all students, boys and girls, to show more understanding of oral communication. As one boy said, "After that stuff we did in class, I can't even sit with my friends or with my family at home without noticing who's making eye contact and who's leading the conversation." That doesn't mean that every individual will *care* enough to change behaviors, but the culture of the class as a whole will be different. There will now be a room full of people *seeing* what's going on with new eyes, paying attention to the quality of communication, with at least some of them taking pride in their ability to do something about unsatisfactory communication.

You can appeal directly to that pride in being a "fixer." With some difficult boys, nothing works as well as taking them aside privately and, instead of scolding, asking them to use their expertise to help out. "You know, I can see your group is having some problems. Susan doesn't feel she's being listened to, and it looks as if Derek is giving up. I think you have the people skills to help fix things in your group and bring them along. Can you help me that way?" Approached that way, one of the most recalcitrant boys in the school looked me in the eye and said confidentially, "Leave it to me, sir." Then he returned to his group and made things better.

I can imagine some teachers saying, "That all sounds fine, but I don't have time to add in a whole unit on group processes. We have too much to cover as it is." Actually, that concern can lead to the very best handling of oral skills. If you can't fit it in as a separate topic, then weave oral communication into the literature curriculum. Many works of literature already deal with communication problems and the failure of community, and it makes sense to address those concerns in ways that connect with our own relationships. What better way to study communication processes than as an integral part of a unit on *Lord of the Flies*, *A Separate Peace*, *Animal Farm*, *Black Boy*, *Ordinary People*, or *One Flew Over the Cuckoo's Nest*?

Listening

The classic complaint leveled by girls and women against boys and men is that they don't listen. Some have suggested that men perhaps listen more than women realize but haven't developed the active listening skills necessary to *signal* the fact that they're listening. They haven't developed the habit of keeping up a stream of feedback by saying "mmm-hmm" or "yeah." They haven't learned to nod and ask gentle encouraging questions. Their response is more likely to be stone-faced, and asking prob- ing questions may even be seen by them as intrusive, with silence being more tactful (Maccoby 1998, 201; Tannen 1990, 142, 59). To the extent that boys really are listening but just don't show it in obvious ways, the remedy, of course, is to teach those skills explicitly and demand that they be practiced in the classroom. At the same time, girls need to learn that listening may look different when it's done by a boy (or someone from another culture), and that silence doesn't always imply unconcern.

Still, for many boys and men, there probably is a deeper attitudinal difficulty, a genuine reluctance to listen. It's not hard to observe that many boys interrupt each other combatively, assert their opinions more defiantly than most girls, and are less likely to pick up and build on some- one else's comment (OFSTED 1993, 16). If boys see life as a contest for status, someone else's contribution to a conversation is likely to be at best a stepping-stone on the road to making one's own point, or, at worst, competition to be squashed. To the extent that this attitude exists, teach- ing the technical skills of looking as if you're listening isn't enough. In- struction also needs to demonstrate the real value of genuine listening: boys have to learn to *want* to listen.

The ability to listen to others with understanding and empathy has been identified as one of the essential "habits of mind" that need to be developed in learners (Costa and Kallick 2000). Relationships break up because people don't listen. Wars break out because whole nations don't listen. As we come to understand how complexly interconnected every- thing in the world is, we realize that no one person can have all the an- swers. We have to be prepared to distribute responsibility for knowledge and intelligence over teams of people, and those team members have to be very good at listening to one another. The ideal of the lone Marlboro Man, silently brooding on the range, is fast becoming archaic.

I like to begin work on listening by asking students to recall some time when they felt they *weren't* being listened to. For themselves, they write a recollection, recalling how they knew someone wasn't listening, how it made them feel, and what they did as a result. (You'll notice that this is an example of *starting* with a feeling response, which is apparently contrary to my advice in Chapter 4 about *delaying* talk about feelings. The difference is that the anger and frustration in these memories is often a good spark for male writing. It's not that hard to write about getting an- noyed at someone not listening to you.)

No one is compelled to share what has been written, but there are always a few people willing to volunteer their memories. Discussion gets rolling and the class begins to construct a list of behaviors that can tip you off that someone isn't listening.

After a while, I show them what the "experts" say about listening and about the roadblocks to real listening. These roadblocks include things like being too ready to jump in with advice, arguing, being sarcastic, judging, or interrogating. (See Costa and Kallick 2000, 78, for a fuller list, or Gordon and Burch 1974, for thorough discussion.) I go on to describe the features of active listening:

- using open, receptive body language
- nodding supportively
- making encouraging sounds ("mmm-hmmm," "aah")
- trying to hear the feelings behind the words
- paraphrasing what the speaker is saying

The last two points need the most work and will be the subjects of the two following sections.

Subtext, Thought Balloons, and Decoding

People aren't always good at realizing that what someone says or does can be a mask for what he or she is really feeling. You and I learn, or ought to learn, that when students arrive in grumpy moods or with an attitude, it doesn't necessarily mean they're annoyed at *us*. Kids—especially boys—don't always understand that. Lots of fights between boys break out because someone tosses out a cheap insult or careless slight, and the receiver takes the insult literally and personally. It's worthwhile spending time teaching kids to look for the message behind the behavior (Browne 1995, 89-91). Boys' interpersonal relationships as well as their understanding of literature will be helped if we can get them to see past the literal or surface levels of life and literature.

One way of using literature to develop such awareness is through the idea of dramatic subtext. Playscripts often have feelings going on beneath the literal surface of language and that level of subtext can be articulated in the classroom by having one set of student actors read the script while a second set of actors shadows the characters, speaking the inner, unspoken thoughts.

The cartoon convention of word balloons can be helpful here as well. Students all know the difference between "talk balloons," and "thought balloons" and comic strips sometimes play on the difference between what is spoken and what is thought. This can be a useful way of representing a character's complexity: draw on the blackboard a representation of the character with a talk balloon and a simultaneous thought balloon. ("Here is what the character says, but here is what he thinks.")

The ability to listen to the thoughts and feelings that lie just beyond what's being said is called *sensitivity* when a woman does it, but you may find it easier to sell the concept to boys if you steer clear of that word, calling it instead the ability to *decode* what's being said. Sending encoded messages is what the military or other institutions do when they're not sure the real message can be safely sent; the same lack of security in personal relationships causes us to suppress or encode our feelings. The decoder has to know how to unlock the real meaning. That whole analogy is appealing to boys, who probably know about encrypted computer messages. Sensitivity, on the other hand, comes from the "soft" world of women and is often used to criticize boys. ("You're so insensitive," spoken by a girl to a guy, is a complaint. "You're so sensitive," spoken by a boy to another boy, is probably a taunt.)

Paraphrasing

When a listener attempts to verbalize his or her understanding of what's behind the words, the speaker may experience the satisfaction of knowing that someone has *really* listened. However, taking the time to paraphrase what someone else has said, or meant to say, isn't a skill that comes naturally, particularly to boys, who are more likely to be waiting impatiently to get on with what they want to say. Just telling kids that something is important doesn't guarantee that they'll buy in to it. To address underlying reluctance to listen, we have to teach listening *experientially*. That means that in addition to presenting the skills, we have to arrange classroom situations in which students will actually *use* the skills and, we hope, thereby *experience* the genuine value of listening.

A good strategy is to designate certain times in class for *active listening discussions,* when anyone wanting to speak has to begin by *paraphrasing* the previous speaker's comments, *to the satisfaction of that speaker.* Students must be taught that a paraphrase isn't a mechanical repetition of someone else's words: they have to put their understanding into their own words, and the first speaker has to be satisfied with the paraphrase. If that speaker feels that he or she hasn't been heard correctly, the turn passes to someone else who may be able to offer a more satisfying paraphrase, or the original speaker may need to have a second try at saying what he or she means.

Inevitably, students are astonished to realize how little they normally listen. Really trying to understand someone else requires so much effort that they find it exhausting. Boys, in particular, unaccustomed to putting their own thoughts on hold while paying attention to another, may be irritated. I suggest not trying to prolong the first session too long. The constant paraphrasing will seem stilted and artificial the first time, but if you regularly include active listening sessions, in time it all becomes easier. The real payoff comes as students experience the benefits of listening and being listened to and gradually begin to like the feeling. At that point, I sometimes notice kids slipping spontaneously and unself-consciously into "active listening mode." As that kind of listening behavior spreads throughout the class, you may sense the culture of the room changing to something that feels much healthier than the competitive attention seeking and arguing that sometimes characterize classrooms.

"Such a Girlie Thing to Say!"

I've taught listening in lots of English classes, but the story I want to tell you now is about another teacher's work with a special education class. I think the story is important because it's such a good example of experiential learning that addresses initial male reluctance—better than any example I can pull out of my own lessons.

Jayne Marshall's grade 11 special education class consists of five boys, all diagnosed with learning disabilities. (The class is all boys not because of any policy of segregation, but because boys always make up the bulk of students identified as learning disabled.)

Jayne's intention is to teach a listening unit much like the one I have described earlier. In the initial discussion, when Jayne asks them to think about an occasion when they wished someone had listened to them, the boys have no difficulty thinking of times when they were angry and wanted to "tell someone off."

Ken tells a story about seeing an older man yelling at kids for no apparent reason. He went over to the man and belligerently demanded, "What are you yelling at me like that for?" Understandably, this provoked an escalation of anger.

Jayne asks Ken, "Did you ever understand why he was angry?"

"No."

"Did you wish you knew?"

"Yeah."

Jayne decides it's time to introduce a model of listening behavior. "Well, you could have said, 'You seem really angry. Is it something I've done?'"

The whole class groans and students roll their eyes. Ken finds this suggestion so ludicrous that his whole body writhes. *"I couldn't say that! That's such a girlie thing to say! I'm a guy. I have to be macho."* (Incidentally, Jayne tells me later that Ken is in fact a caring and polite boy.)

Ken feels he has to clarify what he means by "girlie." "I don't mean like you, Miss. What I mean is that kind of . . . oooOOOooo." He demonstrates a caricature of femininity: a feathery, falsetto voice, a twisted body, and much eyelash batting.

That day's discussion concludes with a chat about the expectations of male behavior.

The next day, Jayne begins by talking about the importance of hearing the feelings, not just the words. The boys seem to understand. On the overhead projector, Jayne shows them examples of roadblocks, the things we say and do instead of listening. She continues to invite examples from their lives, and the boys compete with one another to give colorful examples of when they told people off.

Jayne picks up on one of the complaints. Roger tells the class that he had been doing well in a technology course, but when the tech teacher came down with a long-term illness, no qualified substitute teacher could be found and the course could not continue. The class was converted to a "personal life management" course. It is a miserable situation: Roger feels cheated out of the one subject he could do well in, and he feels little rapport with the new teacher.

Roger is worked up about this situation, he clearly wants to say more, and Jayne begins to set up communication roadblocks. Her strategy is shrewd and deliberate, but Roger doesn't know that yet.

Jayne stands in front of him, her elevation underlining the fact that she speaks as an authority, and defends the school's action.

She uses logic. "It's a legal requirement that you have a course in that time slot," she reminds him. "You know there's a shortage of teachers. What did you expect?" She hands out cheap advice. "You should have just lived with it."

As Jayne piles up roadblocks, Roger gets louder and louder, angrier and angrier. He's not angry at Jayne, but at the situation he is brooding on. He quotes belligerent confrontations between him and the substitute teacher. "So then I said . . . and she said . . ." He becomes nearly incoherent as he leaps from memory to memory.

Then Jayne suddenly turns into a different person. She sits down in a relaxed position beside Roger and says in a quiet voice, "You sound really angry about that." Without announcing it, she has switched into active listening.

Roger sighs and says, "Yeah," now sounding a little tired.

"Seems to me you think that just wasn't fair."

Roger sits back in his chair and goes on to explain in detail what wasn't fair. Jayne says, "Uh huh," several times. Roger's rage is gone. He is simply explaining the essence of the injustices clearly and coherently, and when he is finished, he stops.

Jayne says, "I can see why you'd be upset."

Roger half smiles and nods. "Yeah."

Jayne allows a few moments of silence, then explains how she had deliberately used roadblocks to show their effect. The kids laugh. "Miss, you used him!"

She agrees and apologizes. "And then I did a different kind of listening. Can you tell me what I did?" Because they have been talking about listening for the past few days, they are able to describe what the teacher had done, physically and verbally.

The class goes on to construct, with Jayne, a blackboard list of the signals that tell you when someone is really listening. Then they watch while Jayne role-plays listening to another student talking about a different problem (a "beef"). The class is instructed to watch critically and be prepared to describe evidence of the teacher listening or not listening.

At the end, the kids acknowledge that Jayne has done a good job, but they tell her that at one point she rubbed her eyes. To them, this looked like a turning away, a breaking of eye contact. The student with the beef agrees that at that moment, he wondered if he had said something wrong. Jayne confirms that she was momentarily not listening, but rather thinking of what she was going to say next, which is indeed a roadblock.

Then she invites a student to be the listener while she lays out her own beef. Davinder volunteers, laughing. "Now Miss, this is how the expert does it," he says.

Jayne talks about something that has been happening in school, and Davinder does an excellent job of listening. Then they all take turns doing short rounds of listening to each other, with everyone watching to see how well the listener shows that he is attentive and how well he decodes and paraphrases feelings.

All five boys do the exercise well. This is an observable and remarkable change for boys whose usual response to classroom talk about feelings used to be "I don't know" and a shrug of the shoulders. Their more normal conversational style would be to say, "You goof. That was really stupid," and yet here they are, proving that they can interpret subtle signals of body language, and that they can listen carefully and empathetically to one another—all the things guys aren't supposed to be able to do.

As the class draws to a close, one boy says it's harder to be listened to by another guy.

"Why?" asks Jayne.

"Because it's kinda weird. Guys *don't* listen."

Davinder says, "Yes they do. My friend Greg does. But maybe that's because I've known him forever."

"Yeah, but I've known Pat forever and he just walks off when I'm trying to tell him something."

They decide to have a vote. "Who knows a guy who really listens?" It turns out that no one can think of anyone except the friend that Davinder mentioned.

"Girls will listen and it's really nice," offers Roger. "And they say, 'Awww . . . really?' and then they give you a hug. And then you think real fast of something else to tell them so they'll listen some more and give you another hug." There is laughter.

Looking back at the listening they have done today, Jayne asks, "Did it feel good to be able to talk to someone who was listening like that?"

They all nod and say, "Yeah," looking Jayne straight in the eye, which they often don't do when feelings are being discussed.

Jayne continues, "And when you were the listener, reflecting back those feelings you were hearing, did it feel weird?" They all agree it did but say it was "okay anyway."

The bell sounds. It's lunchtime and they ought to be scrambling out to the cafeteria, but today they linger. The classroom today has been a warm and good place for them.

Of course, with five students, this was an unusually small class. Jayne has been fortunate to develop a special relationship with these boys, working with them closely over three years. This is an advantage that you and I might never have, unless we teach remedial or special education classes like Jayne's. Some of you might point out that this was an all-male class and wonder whether a mixed class would have been as successful. I'm not sure. Still, what happened in that room tells me that it can be done: boys can learn how to listen and they can learn that listening and being listened to feel good.

Those boys haven't had a magical transformation. They'll probably continue to get into name-calling conflicts at home and on the street, and I'm sure they won't always do a good job of listening in school. What has happened, I think, is that they have briefly experienced a larger version of themselves: not a feminized or "girlie" version, but simply a *larger* version of their own humanity. They came into the class with a narrowly restricted view of what a man could say and do. When they left the room, they knew that there was more to be had from speaking and listening than they had known before. They knew that they could tap into that expanded potential. And they knew they would be no less men for doing so.

It seems to me those are pretty fine things for them to learn.

9 Classroom Visit

Grade 9, Academic

Jill Birch is a new, young teacher. I visited her class during the first term of her first year. Some of you reading this are veterans, but you may remember how traumatic those first few months can be, before the novice gains confidence and a reputation. By her second semester, Jill was already a very different (and happier) teacher, who perhaps looked back at these early months as one would recall a nightmare that seemed, at the time, to have no end in sight. What follows is a snapshot of a classroom at a difficult time in a teacher's career. It reflects the behavior we may see from fourteen-year-old boys (and girls) when they find themselves in a crowded room with an inexperienced teacher. At a time when the profession faces many retirements and high turnover, we can expect to see more classrooms that look like this.

There are thirty-one kids in this grade 9 "academic" class; fourteen girls and seventeen boys. Marks in the class are typical of results from around the world. Three months into the course, there are five students with grade A standing, all of them girls. Of the six students who are failing, five are boys.

Jill's work is made more difficult by a fluke of timetabling: both of her grade 9 classes have been scheduled into a room with round tables, seating four students at a table. It's a useful arrangement for group work, as students can collaborate with minimum movement of furniture. On the other hand, it is a treacherous room for a young teacher struggling to hold students' attention, as there are just too many ways for kids not to look at the teacher.

As I find out later, there's another limitation holding Jill back. In her teacher-training program, one professor had warned prospective teachers never to send students to the office for disciplinary action: "If you have to ask for help, the administration will think you're weak." Jill has taken this guidance to heart. It's now the beginning of November, she has never sent a student to the office, her grade 9 classes are disorderly, and she is unhappy.

On the first day of school, students chose their own seats, which meant there were boys' tables and girls' tables. Alarmed by the amount of socializing going on, after two weeks, Jill imposed a new seating plan, with boys and girls spread evenly throughout the room. Disappointingly, it doesn't seem to have made much difference to their concentration.

Jill has been noticing lot of verb inconsistencies in the class' writing, so today she begins with a mini-lesson on verb forms. She writes notes on the blackboard for them to copy, which means her back is often to the class. (Yes, you see it coming, don't you?) It takes only a couple of minutes for two boys at opposite sides of the room to start throwing a paper airplane between each other whenever Jill turns to the board. I particularly notice Ivan, who is sitting closest to me. He is the only student who has ended up at a table by himself, and when he is not throwing the paper airplane, he is busy under his desk, fashioning a sword out of tinfoil.

As the period goes on, more and more boys join in building, flying, and intercepting paper airplanes. At no time do I ever see a girl so much as touch a paper airplane; girls barely even seem to notice the planes floating over their heads. Flight paths are erratic, and a plane sometimes lands near a girl, but there is always a boy ready to snatch it away.

This, however, does not mean that the girls are being attentive students. As far as I can see, almost no one is paying attention to Jill's lesson. The boys are more physically obvious, but at all the tables, students chat happily to each other, barely bothering to lower their voices. While the boys' network encompasses the whole room—words, gestures, and aircraft crossing the length and width of the room—the girls' many networks consist of only two or three other girls—the ones at their own table and maybe at one adjacent table. The girls are highly social, but, unlike the boys, there's no sense that they're communicating with the whole room.

Jill notices all this, of course, and repeatedly calls for attention and for an end to the paper planes, but her voice seems pretty peripheral. At one point, she assigns a short textbook exercise, and most students do at least open their books and go through the motions of doing the work, although the chatting and plane construction continue.

Ivan, sitting by himself at the side, does not open his books, doesn't speak to people at the next table over, and becomes a marvel of industry, creating literally dozens of airplanes over the next hour. His industry, to a large extent, keeps the game alive for the rest of the boys in the class. Later I look in Ivan's official student file, and everything there looks "normal," but the Ivan I see in class is unmistakably different. At first I think he is childishly absorbed in his own world, obsessively folding paper in a private ritual, but then it dawns on me that he's not actually withdrawing, but rather trying to make contact in one clumsy way that he knows well. I never see him chatting with other students, but sending and receiving paper planes is his way of interacting with other boys. In fact, this isolate wields enormous power, in the sense that the airplane game, which he seems to be the driving force behind, dominates the classroom today. He gets contact with others and he gets power, but he's not getting much of an education, either academically or socially. I'm not a therapist, but it's not hard to guess that Ivan needs to learn other, more constructive ways of connecting. As I watch Ivan, I think of William Pollack, the author of *Real Boys* (1998), who says the yearning for connection is a primary urge in everyone, an urge that is often frustrated in boys, who may have inadequate training in positive ways of achieving connections.

After a few minutes, Jill tries to take up the verb exercise. At one point she calls Ivan's name to get his attention. He quickly and unnecessarily exclaims, "I got it done!" This is plainly untrue: I know he hasn't opened the textbook or lifted a pen. Jill probably can't see that from where she stands, and as she turns to another student to carry on with the lesson, I begin to doubt whether Ivan really wants to hide his misdemeanors from the teacher. A lie like that could be so easily disproved, it seems to beg for discovery—a classic, negative, attention-getting ploy. Whereas other boys try to hide what they are doing, throwing planes only when they are sure the teacher is turned away, Ivan's moves are blatant and risky, demanding detection. (Or connection.)

Jill now moves on to the next activity and asks students to reorganize themselves into new groups. Almost all choose same-sex working groups. After most of the shuffling has died down, Ivan conspicuously hasn't made an effort to find a group. (Jill tells me later that most of the students don't want to work with him.) He's still alone at his own table, but he's actually doing schoolwork—not for this class, but rather homework for another course. I can't help wondering whether the pressure of forming social connections has made him retreat into doing schoolwork as a momentary escape. After a couple of minutes, he closes his book and tries to join a group of six boys. They reject him. Jill sends him to another group, which he joins reluctantly, scraping his chair noisily across the floor.

The class will be working on a media studies activity that involves looking through newspapers for stories about the current federal election campaign. Jill gives instructions for preparing group presentations on the stories they find. Students have been told to bring in their own newspapers from home today, but no one has; anticipating this, Jill has brought in her own supply. As she hands out newspapers, several boys shout, "Is the sports section here?" "Hey, there's no sports!" "Me! Me! I want the sports!" Jill grits her teeth.

How is she to understand this? Have they really not heard, not listened to her instructions that made it clear they were getting the *news* section to look for *election* coverage—not sports stories? Do they care so little for her plans that they are loudly announcing they intend to look for something else? Is this a deliberate, rude snub of the topic? Of the teacher? Or is it just thoughtless silliness? Why is it only boys who are so loud about announcing they want to read sports, not anything else? For whom are these outbursts intended? The teacher? The girls? The other guys? (I think mainly the latter.)

One group of six boys seems especially unproductive and loudly off topic. Later, Jill confirms that these are six of the weakest students in the class. This is the group that Ivan had wanted to join, and which had rejected him. It must be painful: he seems to be trying to establish an identity with conspicuous noncompliance, but even the other noncompliant students won't accept him.

Around the room, the airplane throwing has picked up intensity, always just behind the teacher's back. There is one moment when the space over our heads is so thick with aircraft, I am reminded of pictures of London during the Blitz in World War II.

Jill privately approaches Ivan to tell him to lay off the paper planes. His reply is interesting, because he doesn't just say, "Okay," or "Sorry." Instead, he goes way beyond credibility and declares, "I don't know how to make an airplane." This lie is so breathtaking in its immensity that I am now sure Ivan wants to provoke a response from the teacher. Jill doesn't take the bait. She just moves to another student and I suppose she is right to avoid rewarding his provocation. Still, someone needs to give him some kind of attention. Someone needs to sit down with Ivan and lay out what he or she sees, show him what he's doing, and help him figure out other ways of getting attention.

Ten minutes before the end of the class, Ivan seems to have given up on paper airplanes. Instead, he has earphones on and is listening to a portable CD player. Is this a retreat into a private world? It could be, but he has the volume turned so high that I can hear the rattle of his music halfway across the room, even above the considerable din of the rest of the class. The headset is a clear violation of school rules and succeeds in winning the teacher's attention again. This time she takes a chair and escorts Ivan to sit in the hall outside. As Jill returns to class, Ivan darts through the open classroom door and snatches a piece of paper from the recycling box, located just inside the door. The other students begin to clean up, and Jill sternly lectures them about their behavior today. Ivan's arm slips through the open doorway and throws one last plane, which sails gracefully across the front of the room, behind Jill's back, just as she finishes by warning that absolutely no paper airplanes will be tolerated tomorrow.

The next day, I return to see the groups present their findings about the election news stories. They obviously didn't do much work yesterday, and Jill gives them five minutes more to "finish"—in truth, for some of them, to begin—their preparations. Today I'm sitting near a long table shared by two groups. There is a group of four girls who seem to be doing appropriate planning. It's pretty perfunctory, but the teacher assigned the work, so they're going to do it. After a few minutes they finish what they consider to be adequate preparation and begin to chat.

At the other end of the table, three boys huddle together. One of them flips a coin idly as they talk about their favorite music. They grab at the first boy's coin and show off their talent at spinning and flipping coins.

The "five minutes" for final preparation have spun out to fifteen, and now it really is time to see their presentations. As we settle in to see what transpires, I guess Jill's expectations may be similar to mine, somewhere between grim resignation and dread.

The first group up is the all-boy, underachieving group that had rejected Ivan the day before. I know they achieved nothing yesterday, but in today's fifteen minutes, they have pulled themselves together enough to be able to deliver a presentation that has the look of confidence. They are expected to connect their found news story with an article about the media that was read previously by the class. I don't know either the news story or the previous reading, so I'm not able to judge the content, but Jill tells me later their discussion was almost entirely irrelevant, and they seem to have missed the point of both articles. Despite their almost total lack of substance, the boys present with the exuberance of game show contestants.

For them, it is a contest. They want to do better than everyone else, and they see the teacher's follow-up questions as challenges to be overcome. They cheer each other on. ("Good answer!" "Now back to you, John!" "Right on!") When they finish, they call for audience applause. When Jill carefully suggests that their highly tangential news story "may not have been the best choice for this task," one boy belligerently shrugs her off with, "Good enough for me." (Again, I wonder if this is deliberate scorn for the teacher's judgment, or merely thoughtless boorishness.)

Many boys thrive on the risk of last-minute pressure and competition. At its best, this can lead to glorious achievement, but today we have seen a depressing display of those qualities reduced to empty mockeries.

For these boys, the task is all *contest* and no *content*. They strut with stereo-typical male bravado, in effect daring the (female) teacher to find any fault.

The second group to present has three girls and one uncomfortable-looking boy. Their insights aren't brilliant, but they have done what they were supposed to do, and it quickly becomes clear to everyone that they are doing a much better job than the previous group. This brings out the combative instincts in the first group, who, from their seats now, attack the second group with questions that have the apparent form of class-room talk, echoing Jill's challenges to them a few minutes earlier. The difference is that the boys use the questions as assault weapons, with unveiled hostility.

"What's the writer's point of view?"

"What's the relevance to the media article we read?"

"What's your main point?"

As the second group returns to its table, a boy from the first group loudly announces, "Ours was way better than that," and the boys begin pestering Jill to announce the marks of the groups after each presenta-tion. She refuses.

It goes on. Four girls get up; they keep their eyes glued on the teacher as they quickly deliver an appropriate commentary. They are dutiful but obviously want to get back to their seats before those boys close in for the kill.

Ivan's group follows—four boys with brief notes on one crumpled piece of paper. It seems that only two of them have prepared the task. They pass the page to the other two, who read out prearranged segments uncomprehendingly, as if sounding out a foreign language.

Then the girls who are at the table near me go to the front and speak articulately and briefly. Like the previous girl group, they are determined to make eye contact with no one but the teacher. After that first group, everyone is in a hurry. Girl groups in particular seem eager to escape the combative situation that the boys are trying to create and control.

The last group is interrupted when Jill angrily has to remove a news-paper from Ivan's hands: he has been ripping the paper apart and Jill needs it for her next class.

Finally, the presentations are over and the students return to their regular seating.

Then, just before the end of the period, a tall and confident girl enters, late. Everything stops and all eyes turn to her. She has braids in her hair.

A handful of boys hoot, "Ooooh! Where have you been?"

"Look at her hair!"

A couple of girls get up and hug the new arrival as she finds her seat. They welcome her with gentle warmth, pulling out a chair for her and touching her arm. It is a strange contrast to the lassitude, wariness, grudging compliance, and taunting that I've been watching for the last half hour. Later, Jill tells me that this is one of the best students in the class, who has just returned today from three weeks of family vacation in the Middle East.

I suppose no one would hug Ivan if he were to return from three weeks' absence.

The picture I have painted of this class is not appealing, but it is true. It demonstrates a number of the most extreme gender stereotypes. The boys with their disruptions, their large-scale attention seeking, their resistance, their thoughtlessness, their appetite for competition, and the girls with their small social clusters, their willingness to do what the teacher asks, their anxious discomfort with public speaking and combat, and the open display of warm affection for a friend—all this reads like a textbook list of generic male/female characteristics, with the boys cast in a particularly unfavorable light. I'd love to be able to explode all these stereotypes, but I can't. It's real. Classes like this go on all the time.

The boys described here aren't deviants and delinquents. They are middle-class kids, mainly from "good homes." Most of them are decent people to talk to one-on-one. Most will go to university and be at least moderately successful. They will become accountants, doctors, fathers, lawyers, actors, engineers, and teachers. What I saw in my visit is what boys and girls can be like at age fourteen. They can be like this if the chemistry—the particular mix of personalities, classroom activity, and teacher capacity—is wrong. The result, obviously, is that these teenagers aren't getting the education that Jill or you or I or their parents would want for them.

It can be like this, but it doesn't have to be. Kids have lots of potential, good and bad, and we have to recognize *both* faces of that potential, which is why I needed to describe this class for you. At this point in her career, dealing with the constraints I mentioned at the outset, Jill couldn't help but let things slide into a nightmare. This book is about some of the ways we can fight that slide and help all our students—boys and girls—become more than stereotypes of their genders.

10 *An Infinity of Possibilities*

To anyone who works with teenagers, it comes as no surprise to point out that identity formation is a crucial—perhaps *the* crucial—challenge of adolescence. Sometimes adolescents generate multiple identities and metamorphose between them with astonishing speed, like a shape-shifting mythical creature. Of course, we all juggle multiple selves as we engage the several roles we have in life, but the adolescent struggle can be particularly bewildering, both to themselves and to their parents. As we grow older, I suppose we sand down some of the rougher edges of our layered identities. We relax and learn to live with our internal contradictions, but that hasn't happened yet for teenagers. They want the world and themselves to make sense *now*, and they think they should be able to find "the real me" somewhere in the cacophony of inner voices (Harter, Waters, and Whitesell 1997, 153).

In the end, identity consolidation isn't a matter of locking in on just one possible identity. Instead, we build and learn to hold in mind a more complex, multifaceted notion of self. What had been an incoherent, simplistic, or fragmented understanding grows into a more richly complicated construction.

It is an act of interpretation: we interpret ourselves. That's why English teachers can play an important role in the lives of teenagers, for interpretation is our specialty. Dennis Sumara puts this well:

> It seems to me that all teachers must help their students to learn and to continue to develop interpretation practices that help them to negotiate the untidy topography of their own subjectivities. . . . The challenge for secondary English language arts teachers (and, really, for all teachers) is to help our students learn to complicate and complexify their interpretation practices—to help them imagine new possibilities for themselves. (2000, 132)

There is reason for hope here. There ought to be a happy marriage of teenagers' need for self-interpretation and our conceptual tools. In this final chapter, I examine some of the ways in which teachers can play a role in helping students, particularly boys, interpret themselves as gendered beings.

Reviving Laertes Too

In *Reviving Ophelia* (1994), Mary Pipher asks us to recall Shakespeare's Ophelia, who has no sense of inner direction and eventually turns to madness and suicide when the men she is trying to please—Hamlet and her father—pull her in contradictory directions. Pipher sees adolescent girls today, like Ophelia, losing themselves in the contradictory demands made of young women: "achieve, but not too much; be polite, but be yourself" and so on, all at "considerable cost to their humanity" (44). Pipher, in her practice as a therapist, sees girls who become "'female impersonators,' who fit their whole selves into small, crowded spaces" (22).

Pipher's interest is in girls, but much of her analysis could be adapted to boys. Boys too are torn by conflicting pressures to be, on the one hand, traditional strong, independent, tough men and, on the other hand, sensitive, caring, New Age guys. William Pollack describes an experiment in which he gave boys statements that fit either the "macho" image or the "New Age" image. It turned out that most boys agreed with *both* sets of statements, even though it's impossible to be all those contradictory things at the same time. I suppose this could be optimistically read as a sign that boys are embracing diversity, but Pollack is probably closer to the truth when he takes these results as a sign of 'boys' inner unconscious confusion about what society expects of them as males" (1998, 166).

Some girls may become female impersonators, but I also see boys who have become male impersonators. In Chapter 4, I mentioned Rahim, the class clown. With his small body, Rahim seemed to work overtime at trying to fit a mask of hard masculinity onto his cute-as-a-puppy face. When we discussed the issue of violence in media, he was adamant in his unreasoning defense of wrestling and other violent entertainments. Someone mentioned the theory that whoever holds the television's remote control is the one who has family power, and that sparked Rahim to proclaim, "When I'm in the room, I take the remote." When a puzzled girl asked why, Rahim proudly jabbed his thumb into his chest and declared, "Because I'm me." It was a wholly committed performance of macho bravado.

William Pollack writes chillingly about this mask of masculinity:

Unfortunately, at times we all believe the mask because it fits so well and is worn so often it becomes more than just a barrier to genuine commu-

nication or intimacy. The tragedy is that the mask can actually become impossible to remove, leaving boys emotionally hollowed out and vulnerable to failure at school, depression, substance abuse, violence, even suicide. (1998, 15)

In the early years of high school, some boys are especially likely to take up with friends who reflect back to them extreme versions of this tough image, which makes them likely to experiment with high-risk behaviors. Later in the year, I noticed that Rahim had made friends with one of the "baddest" kids in the school, a jail-bitten, drug-addled, walking nightmare. Rahim was well on his way to losing himself, just as surely as any of Pipher's Ophelias.

Shakespeare's Ophelia has a brother, Laertes, who has his own problems with identity switching. Consider the many faces of Laertes. He tries to be a big brother advisor to his sister but has to change roles quickly and become the dutiful son to his father. He goes off to play the scholar but returns with sword in hand, vowing vengeance for his father's death. This is the point at which Laertes is most dangerous and most vulnerable. He yells and swaggers around the palace and the graveyard, delivering a predictable performance of "in your face" manly indignation. He's ready to fight anyone and turn this into an old-fashioned revenge tragedy. He is also innocently susceptible to the wiles of Claudius, who is the more deeply dangerous man, clever with words and able to manipulate the young hothead, conscripting him as a skulking conspirator. In his final scene, Laertes finds yet another self. He repudiates both the vengeful, violent self and the sneaking plotter and becomes instead the forgiving man of honor, but it is too late. By the end, he is just as dead as his sister.

Writers like Mary Pipher have done important work in drawing our attention to the drowning Ophelia. Now we need to think about reviving Laertes, too.

Mirror, Mirror . . .

There is a stage in early adolescence when boys and girls may spend hours in front of their mirrors, testing different expressions, hairstyles, dress, and adornments, and scrutinizing real or imagined physical defects. They gaze at their own images, trying to fathom how others might see them. In an adult, such a habit would be judged mere vanity, but we're probably more forgiving of the fourteen- or fifteen-year-old at the mirror. We sense this is no mere self-admiration. For that teenager, there may be a good deal of painful self-criticism, as well as a more nebulous quest to understand what that image in the mirror means, what it says about who he or she is.

There is more than one kind of mirror. Another kind of mirroring takes place in the early adolescent tendency to define the world of their peers by stereotypical labels. As Eli Newberger points out, this simplistic world of "jocks, brains, nerds, dweebs, druggies, toughs, normals, preppies" and so on gives teenagers the feedback they need as they try to figure out where they fit into the social landscape (1999, 229).

Yet another mirror can be found in mass media and popular culture. It's an odd sort of mirror, of course. Media images are all constructed by someone else, usually by someone much older than the kids themselves and usually someone with an interest in making money. Still, those producers would say they are giving the audience what it wants, "mirroring" the interests, fears, and aspirations of young people. This media-constructed hall of mirrors is the world in which teenagers swim like fish, perfectly at home, often, like fish, taking for granted the element in which they move, not stopping to ask critical questions about the images that define their culture.

I see media studies as an important component of the English program. If our mandate is to study how cultural meanings are made, then we have to look at the meanings that are made every day around our students. In particular, if we want students to understand how gender is constructed, they need to look at the powerful cultural forces that shape images of men and women, delineating the possibilities they are able to imagine for themselves.

The most straightforward and possibly most useful media studies exercise is simply to collect a series of media artifacts and ask what kinds of roles appear for men and for women. These artifacts might include clips from movies (perhaps representing several decades or different genres), popular TV shows, music videos and lyrics, comic books, magazines, and advertisements in various media. You can narrow or broaden the range of materials to suit the interests and abilities of your classes. As they examine these artifacts, students can catalog their findings through asking questions such as the following.

- What kinds of activities do we find men doing? What are women doing?
- What are we supposed to admire in men? In women?
- What are we expected to find laughable in men? In women?
- What does it seem a man should fear? What should a woman fear?
- What do winning and losing look like for men? For women?

As this study progresses, it is natural to note the fairly narrow range of possibilities offered by many media sources, as well as their distance from real-life experiences, and to consider the effects of spending a lifetime looking into these "mirrors."

In *Challenging Macho Values* (1996), Jonathan Salisbury and David Jackson suggest similar strategies for media study, including an entertaining activity in which aliens try to figure out what the behavior of male earthlings is all about (164). Salisbury and Jackson's lessons, designed for all-male settings, look only at men's behavior, but their suggestions can easily be adapted to include both male and female images. In fact, I would caution teachers that this work in mixed-sex classrooms *must* look at both sexes. "Gender studies" has for too long meant only women's studies, which has been an irritant to some men and boys. We don't want to create an imbalance in the other direction by suggesting that only men have identity issues.

You could, of course, arrive in class with a very specific set of categories to guide student investigation for each of those questions, but I wouldn't. Do you remember those Japanese math classrooms I mentioned in Chapter 6? The key to their success was the way teachers insisted that students take responsibility for creating categories and procedures—in other words, insisting that students think like mathematicians. Similarly, it should be the students, not the teachers, who are doing the work of thinking like cultural analysts. *They*, the students, can come up with labels to describe the range of roles available to men and women in the media. If they do this work in small groups, there will probably be differences between the categories created by different groups. That's fine, because such differences also appear when adult commentators try to describe what they see in the media.

If you'd like to supplement student research with professionally prepared materials, I can recommend a couple of videotapes. *Killing Us Softly 3* (2000) examines images of women in advertising, and *Tough Guise* (1999) offers a hard-hitting analysis of masculinity in today's culture. More recent resources may be available by the time you read this.

You'll notice that, a few paragraphs ago, I used the phrase "mass media and popular culture." By "popular culture," I mean something a little larger than media products. Under this heading we can include all the practices that define a culture: festivals, eating habits, manners, play, toys, sports, clothing, dating rituals, and pastimes. There's plenty of room here for cultural investigations that students find genuinely interesting, and it's not hard to raise questions about gender roles in any of those topics.

To give just one example, an examination of children's toys raises interesting questions about the roles children are encouraged to rehearse. An inquiry can begin by simply asking students to bring in a favorite toy from childhood. We have now supposedly had the benefit of several decades of feminist influence, but the girls' aisle of toy stores is still a blaze of pink, full of stoves and babies, while the boys' aisle is full of action figures with murderous intent. Even as Barbie became thinner over the years, boys' action figures have grown bigger and bigger muscles. The first G. I. Joe figure, introduced in 1964, had realistic proportions, but, over the years, G. I. Joe has become implausibly muscular. Similar growth patterns appear in other figures, like Batman, Wolverine, and Luke Skywalker, as well as in the live men who perform for the World Wrestling Federation. This trend has been linked to American boys and men becoming worried about body image and dedicated to a hypermasculine ideal that can be achieved only by steroid use and obsessive workouts at the gym (Pope, Phillips, and Olivardia 2000, 40–44).

Another way of tapping in to popular culture is by asking students to come up with all the gender clichés, stereotypes, and familiar sayings they can think of—"men are good at mechanical stuff," "women are better with children," "men don't cry," "women are more emotional," and so on—and then having them sort these sayings into *dominant, emergent,* or *residual* beliefs. (These categories are derived from Raymond Williams [1977].)

1. *Dominant beliefs*: These are the widely held, mainstream, "politically correct" beliefs that you can safely say in public without any fear of offending people. For example, "Women and men deserve equal career opportunities."

2. *Residual beliefs*: These beliefs reflect earlier versions of society and were dominant at one time, but can't be publicly spoken today without embarrassment. Nevertheless, they may continue to hold great residual power. Few people today would openly say that "men are better suited to run governments," but the overwhelming number of men elected to powerful positions suggests that the old belief has not disappeared.

3. *Emergent beliefs*: These are ideas that are starting to be held by some people but are still considered extreme or radical. As time passes, they may work their way into the mainstream and become dominant, or they may fade and be remembered only as fads. Emergent beliefs today would include the idea that "homosexuals should be able to have same-sex marriages and enjoy all the legal rights of heterosexual couples."

I've used this approach with students in grades 11 and 12. I find that thinking in terms of these categories prevents students from getting stuck in pointless quarrels—for example, about whether women are in fact as good as men in government—in which they might only be digging their entrenched positions more deeply. Instead, everyone can step back and look at the whole cultural system of values and see how it works. Students can see that our values have a cultural history behind them and that at least some of our belief systems are in flux. (I say, "at least some. . . ." If you teach in a religious school, you would probably raise the question of whether certain beliefs are exempt from this evolution.)

One benefit of gender work through media studies is that students may come to see that our understandings of gender are not always based on essential, intrinsic qualities in the two sexes. Rather, masculinity and femininity are, to some extent, *constructions*, and we can see this construction taking place when we examine gender imagery in the media. When we analyze our beliefs in terms of the residual/dominant/emergent spectrum, we realize that those constructions change over time, historically. Indeed, in our own time, they seem to be changing fairly quickly. Gender performances also evolve at the individual level as we work our way through our daily lives, rethinking how to be a man or a woman. To be aware of that fluidity is to see our own time as an exciting moment in cultural history and to see our individual existence as a source of possibilities, rather than a fixed stance.

I'm sure some teachers who feel uncertain about media study will be more confident approaching gender issues through literature, using the same questions (from earlier) that we might apply to the media. In many familiar works, it's not hard to see that the nature of masculinity and femininity is an issue worth pursuing. *Macbeth*, for example, hinges on the question of what it takes to be a man, and the word echoes through the play. (Lady Macbeth knows the power of an appeal to her husband's masculinity. Her ultimate argument is, in effect, "If you were a man, you'd do it." Later, Macduff knows that he has to both fight and feel like a man.) In *Henry IV, Part I*, Prince Hal works his way through a process of identity clarification, as he figures out how to incorporate the different male role models in his life—his father the statesman, Falstaff the reveler, and Hotspur the warrior—eventually transcending the narrowness of each to achieve a flexible blend of their best qualities. In *To Kill a Mockingbird*, being a girl is an issue for Scout, and the men in the book display a wide range of masculine behaviors and attitudes. *The Outsiders*, *Of Mice and Men*, *Huckleberry Finn*, *Julius Caesar*, *The Pearl* . . . there's no shortage of literature suitable for a classroom investigation of masculinity.

Teachers as Mirrors

Popular culture and literature offer images of masculinity that can be studied in class, but there is one more important kind of mirror. Teachers are mirrors too, because the way we treat our students tells them what we expect of them, what we fear of them, and what we allow ourselves to hope and imagine for them. A British report on boys in school found that "a key factor in the attitude of boys was the relationship with, and performance of, the teacher" (QCA 1998, 33).

At a time when community, church, and family ties are weakening, teachers remain important contact points with the adult world. We continue to hold the enormous responsibility of inducting young people into literate adulthood. More than any specific lesson, our daily attitude tells them, "This is what it means to be literate," and "This is what you can be." That attitude also sends signals about what it means to be a man or a woman.

This raises the issue of the teacher's sex, and we know that most English classrooms are staffed by women. When math teachers wanted to do something about girls' attitudes, part of their strategy was the recruitment of more women into the teaching of math. Of course, it would be healthy to show kids that both men and women take an interest in all subjects. Still, we don't want to make the mistake of assuming that just putting a man in the English classroom will automatically make things better for boys. I would always want my own son to have *good* teachers, regardless of their sex. Rather than aiming for a quota of male English teachers, I would rather make sure that *all* teachers—male and female—have enough understanding of the issues to be able to do good work with both boys and girls.

I suppose we might call this understanding "gender consciousness." It implies not only being aware of how student gender affects learning but also being aware of our own gendered preferences. We want to take advantage of students' preferred styles *but also* push them to try other styles. In exactly the same way, we should make the most of our own masculine or feminine teaching styles, *but also* push ourselves to try out "the other way." Like those boys who learned about active listening in Jayne Marshall's class (in Chapter 8), we may find that another way of teaching feels "weird" at first but is "okay anyway."

Some studies have raised interesting questions about gendered teaching styles. (See, for example, Mac an Ghaill [1994] and Skelton [2001].) Martin Nystrand and Adam Gamoran studied hundreds of grade 8 and 9 English lessons over two years, looking especially for the quality of communication that was occurring. They found that some teachers had a notion of "discussion" best described as "forensic":

One teacher, who taught academically talented ninth-grade English in a large urban school, believed that schooling too much favors docile, cooperative students; in contrast, he liked aggressively expressive, openly assertive students who could readily state and defend their points of view and were willing to argue in class, even with him. Right answers weren't enough in his classes, he said; students had to be able to support them and prevail. Needless to say, this conception of discussion as debate favored the most confident, verbally articulate, and competitive of students. This was a view . . . expressed almost exclusively by male teachers. *(1997, 49; emphasis added)*

I don't think this is a bad style of discussion, but this debate-oriented competition to "prevail" is unmistakably masculine and many women don't instinctively feel confrontation to be an appropriate conversational stance (Tannen 1990, 144).

One of my own male colleagues observed that some boys respond well to male English teachers because men are more likely to welcome forceful classroom challenges. On the whole, he's probably right. However, if that's the *only* or the *main* type of discussion that goes on in those classrooms, students (including many girls) who don't feel comfortable with that sparring, intellectual head-butting style may have difficulty connecting with the subject. Others (including many boys) who do enjoy debating are perhaps not being encouraged to try out different approaches to discussion, including "connected," "thinking together" styles of conversation that are sometimes associated with women, as described in *Women's Ways of Knowing* (Belenky et al. 1997). If we reach out to all kinds of students, all have a better chance of growing. In order to do that reaching, we need to be aware of the role of gender in our own communication.

An Australian researcher (Kelly-Byrne 1991) tracked two teachers—one male, one female—teaching the "same" grade 10 curriculum over the course of a year. She doesn't claim that her two subjects represent all teachers, but her findings are interesting nonetheless. The male teacher disavowed gender consciousness, declaring that gender was "not an issue" in his classroom. In fact, in that room, the researcher found a "male-dominated world" where girls had to struggle to be heard. There were contests that created rowdy fun for the boys but had little interest for the girls. There was a highly rule-driven, almost formulaic approach to writing (49–53). Both the teacher and the boys engaged in verbal dueling and joking that sometimes had a sexist edge (96). In the female teacher's classroom, on the other hand, boys were less successful at dominating the agenda and there was greater emphasis on conventional feminine values of "behaving politely, speaking nicely, [and] writing beautifully" (90). Arguably, gender, including the teacher's gender, most emphatically was an issue in both classrooms, but it's not clear that having a man in the classroom served those students any better than having a female teacher.

Accommodating boys' learning styles shouldn't mean simply reinforcing stereotypical male behavior.

For students, especially in the early years of secondary school, we *are* the subject. "English" can only be known by what English teachers do. We are double mirrors, reflecting the kinds of discourse that the subject allows, as well as reflecting back to the students their own possible roles within that discourse. For that reason, we must think carefully about the nature of the classroom contexts we are creating and the gender roles we are ourselves enacting (Hurrell 2000, 20).

Paying attention to gender issues in the media, in literature, in our own teaching, and in our students' learning offers special hope for boys' education if it can begin to shake loose that fixed hold that gender definitions may have on their thinking. As we have seen, teenage boys are particularly likely to deal with the challenge of identity formation by prematurely locking into stereotypical definitions of masculinity. This has been called "foreclosure": avoiding the complexity of life decisions by clinging dogmatically to a narrowed understanding of themselves (Head 1999, 27–28). This understanding is likely to be characterized by rejection of anything identified as feminine. That means rejection of things like reading, the expression of softer feelings, empathetic listening and understanding, and connected rather than competitive work.

We want to move beyond the complacent acceptance that "that's just the way guys are." In the mirror that schools hold up, we want boys to see that there are many ways of being a man, just as there are many ways of being a woman. As Rob and Pam Gilbert say in *Masculinity Goes to School*:

> *Multiple masculinities are . . . multiple possibilities opened up in our culture which expand rather than constrain the opportunities for men to live rewarding lives for themselves and others. (1998, 49)*

Of course, opening up new opportunities for large numbers of our population does disturb the status quo. We should expect resistance, even from those we are most trying to help. It is not easy to find yourself and your world changing. There is security in the stereotype and risk in change. Jerome Bruner writes:

> *Education is risky, for it fuels the sense of possibility. But a failure to equip minds with the skills for understanding and feeling and acting in the cultural world is not simply scoring a pedagogical zero. It risks creating alienation, defiance, and practical incompetence. And all of these undermine the viability of a culture. (1996, 42–43)*

"Alienation, defiance, and practical incompetence": that's not a bad way of describing the condition of many young men in our communities and in our English classrooms.

But it doesn't have to be that way. It can change, and the change can start with teachers, and with the boys and girls in our classes, today.

Works Cited

American Association of University Women (AAUW). 1998. *Gender Gaps: Where Schools Still Fail Our Children*. Executive Summary. Washington: American Association of University Women Educational Foundation.

Applebee, Arthur N. 1993. *Literature in the Secondary School: Studies of Curriculum and Instruction in the United States*. Urbana, IL: National Council of Teachers of English.

———. 1996. *Curriculum as Conversation: Transforming Traditions of Teaching and Learning*. Chicago: University of Chicago Press.

Appleman, Deborah. 2000. *Critical Encounters in High School English: Teaching Literary Theory to Adolescents*. New York: Teachers College Press, and Urbana, IL: National Council of Teachers of English.

Arnot, Madeleine, John Gray, Mary James, Jean Rudduck, with Gerard Duveen. 1998. *Recent Research on Gender and Educational Performance*. Office for Standards in Education. London: The Stationery Office.

Belenky, Mary Field, Blythe McVicker Clinchy, Nancy Rule Goldberger, and Jill Mattuck Tarule. 1997. *Women's Ways of Knowing: The Development of Self, Voice, and Mind*. 10th anniversary ed. New York: Basic.

Bleach, Kevan. 1998a. "What Difference Does It Make? Factors Influencing Motivation and Performance of Year 8 Boys in a Walsall Comprehensive School." In *Raising Boys' Achievement in Schools*, ed. Kevan Bleach. Stoke on Trent: Trentham.

———. 1998b. "Why the Likely Lads Lag Behind: An Examination of Reasons for Some Boys' Poor Academic Performance and Behavior in School." In *Raising Boys' Achievement in Schools*, ed. Kevan Bleach. Stoke on Trent: Trentham.

Boal, Augusto. 1992. *Games for Actors and Non-Actors*. Trans. Adrian Jackson. New York: Routledge.

Bowman, Cynthia Ann. 1992. "Gender Differences in Response to Literature." In *Gender Issues in the Teaching of English*, ed. Nancy Mellin McCracken and Bruce C. Appleby. Portsmouth, NH: Boynton/Cook.

Browne, Rollo. 1995. "Working with Boys and Masculinity." In *Boys in Schools: Addressing the Real Issues—Behavior, Values and Relationships*, ed. Rollo Browne and Richard Fletcher. Sydney: Finch.

Bruner, Jerome. 1996. *The Culture of Education*. Cambridge, MA: Harvard University Press.

Bussière, Patrick, Fernando Cartwright, Robert Crocker, Xin Ma, Jillian Oderkirk, and Yanhong Zhang. 2001. *Measuring up: The Performance of Canada's Youth in Reading, Mathematics and Science*. Ottawa: Statistics Canada.

Cameron, Deborah. 1997. "Performing Gender Identity: Young Men's Talk and the Construction of Heterosexual Masculinity." In *Language and Masculinity*, ed. Sally Johnson and Ulrike Hanna Meinhof. Oxford: Blackwell.

Coates, Jennifer. 1997. "One-at-a-Time: The Organization of Men's Talk." In *Language and Masculinity*, ed. Sally Johnson and Ulrike Hanna Meinhof. Oxford: Blackwell.

Connell, R. W. 1995. *Masculinities: Knowledge, Power and Social Change*. Berkeley and Los Angeles: University of California Press.

———. 2000. *The Men and the Boys*. Berkeley and Los Angeles: University of California Press.

Corson, David. 2001. *Language Diversity and Education*. Mahwah, NJ: Lawrence Erlbaum.

Costa, Arthur L., and Bena Kallick. 2000. "Teaching the Habits of Mind Directly." In *Activating and Engaging Habits of Mind*, ed. Arthur L. Costa and Bena Kallick. Alexandria, VA: Association for Supervision and Curriculum Development.

Education Quality and Accountability Office (EQAO). 2001a. *Contextual Information: The Ontario Secondary School Literacy Test, October 2000*. Toronto: EQAO.

———. 2001b. *Results by Gender—English: The Ontario Secondary School Literacy Test, October 2000*. Toronto: EQAO.

Evans, Alan. 1996. "Perils of Ignoring Our Lost Boys." *Times Educational Supplement* (London): 28 June.

Frater, Graham. 1998. "Boys and Literacy: Effective Practice in Fourteen Secondary Schools." In *Raising Boys' Achievement in Schools*, ed. Kevan Bleach. Stoke on Trent: Trentham.

Freedman, Aviva, and Jennie St-Martin. 2000. "The Computer in the Writing Class." In *Advocating Change: Contemporary Issues in Subject English*, ed. Barrie R. C. Barrell and Roberta F. Hammett. Toronto: Irwin.

Gilbert, Rob, and Pam Gilbert. 1998. *Masculinity Goes to School*. London: Routledge.

Gilligan, Carol. 1982. *In a Different Voice: Psychological Theory and Women's Development*. Cambridge, MA: Harvard University Press.

Goleman, Daniel. 1995. *Emotional Intelligence*. New York: Bantam.

———. 1998. *Working with Emotional Intelligence*. New York: Bantam.

Gordon, Thomas, with Noel Burch. 1974. *Teacher Effectiveness Training*. New York: David McKay.

Grima, Grace. 1999. "Influences of Group Gender Composition on Group Work: A New Zealand Perspective." Paper presented at the joint conference of the Australian Association for Research in Education and the New Zealand Association for Research in Education, 29 November–2 December, Melbourne, Australia.

Gurian, Michael. 1996. *The Wonder of Boys: What Parents, Mentors, and Educators Can Do to Shape Boys into Exceptional Men*. New York: Jeremy P. Tarcher/ Putnam.

———. 1998. *A Fine Young Man: What Parents, Mentors, and Educators Can Do to Shape Adolescent Boys into Exceptional Men*. New York: Jeremy P. Tarcher/Putnam.

Gurian, Michael, and Patricia Henley, with Terry Trueman. 2001. *Boys and Girls Learn Differently! A Guide for Teachers and Parents*. San Francisco: Jossey-Bass/ Wiley.

Hall, Christine, and Martin Coles. 1997. "Gendered Readings: Helping Boys Develop as Critical Readers." *Gender and Education* 9.1: 61–68.

Hamel, Frederick L., and Michael W. Smith. 1998. "You Can't Play If You Don't Know the Rules: Interpretive Conventions and the Teaching of Literature to Students in Lower-Track Classes. *Reading & Writing Quarterly* 14: 355–77.

Harter, Susan, Patricia L. Waters, and Nancy R. Whitesell. 1997. "Lack of Voice as a Manifestation of False Self-Behavior Among Adolescents: The School Setting as a Stage Upon Which the Drama of Authenticity is Enacted." *Educational Psychologist* 32.3: 153–73.

Head, John. 1999. *Understanding the Boys: Issues of Behavior and Achievement*. London: Falmer.

Hurrell, Greg. 2000. "Masculinities in the English Classroom: Looking for Cracks and Fissures in the Stereotypes." Paper presented at the conference of the Australian Association for Research in Education, 4–7 December, Sydney, Australia.

Hyerle, David. 2000. "Thinking Maps: Visual Tools for Activating Habits of Mind." In *Activating and Engaging Habits of Mind*, ed. Arthur L. Costa and Bena Kallick. Alexandria, VA: Association for Supervision and Curriculum Development.

Johnson, Sally. 1997. "Theorizing Language and Masculinity: A Feminist Perspective." In *Language and Masculinity*, ed. Sally Johnson and Ulrike Hanna Meinhof. Oxford: Blackwell.

Kelley, John. 2001. "Gender Breakdown in NCTE's Secondary Section." Email to the author. 29 January.

Kelly-Byrne, Diana. 1991. *The Gendered Framing of English Teaching: A Selective Case Study*. Melbourne: Deakin University Press.

Killing Us Softly 3: Advertising's Image of Women, with Jean Kilbourne. 2000. Dir. Sut Jhally. Northampton, MA: Media Education Foundation.

Kindlon, Dan, and Michael Thompson. 1999. *Raising Cain: Protecting the Emotional Life of Boys*. New York: Ballantine.

Langer, Ellen J. 1997. *The Power of Mindful Learning*. New York: Addison-Wesley.

Mac an Ghaill, Máirtín. 1994. *The Making of Men: Masculinities, Sexualities and Schooling*. Buckingham: Open University Press.

Maccoby, Eleanor E. 1998. *The Two Sexes: Growing Up Apart, Coming Together*. Cambridge, MA: Belknap-Harvard University Press.

Mackey, Margaret. 2000. "Developing Critical Responses to Stories in Many Media." In *Advocating Change: Contemporary Issues in Subject English*, ed. Barrie R. C. Barrell and Roberta F. Hammett. Toronto: Irwin.

Martino, Wayne. 1995. "It's Not the Way Guys Think!" In *Boys in Schools: Addressing the Real Issues—Behavior, Values and Relationships*, ed. Rollo Browne and Richard Fletcher. Sydney: Finch.

Marzano, Robert J., Ronald S. Brandt, Carolyn Sue Hughes, Beau Fly Jones, Barbara Z. Presseisen, Stuart C. Rankin, and Charles Suhor. 1988. *Dimensions of Thinking: A Framework for Curriculum and Instruction*. Alexandria, VA: Association for Supervision and Curriculum Development.

Marzano, Robert J., Debra J. Pickering, and Jane E. Pollock. 2001. *Classroom Instruction That Works: Research-Based Strategies for Increasing Stu-*

dent Achievement. Alexandria, VA: Association for Supervision and Curriculum Development.

Matthews, Brian. 1998. "Co-education, Boys, Girls and Achievement." In *Raising Boys' Achievement in Schools,* ed. Kevan Bleach. Stoke on Trent: Trentham.

McLaren, Christie. 1981. "Suitcase Lady Holds a Package of Dreams." *The Globe and Mail* (Toronto) 24 January. Reprinted as "Suitcase Lady" in *The Act of Writing: Canadian Essays for Composition,* ed. Ronald Conrad. Rev. 3d ed. Toronto: McGraw-Hill Ryerson, 1993.

Millard, Elaine. 1997. *Differently Literate: Boys, Girls and the Schooling of Literacy.* London: Falmer.

Moir, Anne, and David Jessel. 1991. *Brainsex: The Real Difference Between Men and Women.* London: Mandarin.

Myers, Miles. 1996. *Changing Our Minds: Negotiating English and Literacy.* Urbana, IL: National Council of Teachers of English.

National Center for Education Statistics (NCES). 1998. *The 1994 High School Transcript Study Tabulation: Comparative Data on Credits Earned and Demographics for 1994, 1990, 1987, and 1982 High School Graduates.* Rev. By Stanley Legum, Nancy Caldwell, Bryan Davis, Jacqueline Haynes, Telford J. Hill, Stephen Litavecz, Lou Rizzo, Keith Rust, and Ngoan Vo. National Center for Education Statistics, NCES 98-532. Washington, D.C.: U.S. Department of Education.

———. 1999. *NAEP 1998 Writing Report Card Highlights.* National Center for Education Statistics, NCES 1999–464. Washington, D.C.: U.S. Department of Education.

———. 2000. *NAEP 1999 Trends in Academic Progress: Three Decades of Student Performance.* By J. R. Campbell, C. M. Hombo, and J. Mazzeo. National Center for Education Statistics, NCES 2000–469. Washington, D.C.: U.S. Department of Education.

———. 2001. *Digest of Education Statistics, 2000.* By Thomas D. Snyder and Charlene M. Hoffman. National Center for Education Statistics, NCES 2001–034. Washington, D.C.: U.S. Department of Education.

Newberger, Eli H. 1999. *The Men They Will Become: The Nature and Nurture of Male Character.* Cambridge, MA: Perseus.

Nystrand, Martin, and Adam Gamoran. 1997. "The Big Picture: Language and Learning in Hundreds of English Lessons." In *Opening Dialogue: Understanding the Dynamics of Language and Learning in the English Classroom,* ed. Martin Nystrand, with Adam Gamoran, Robert Kachur, and Catherine Prendergast. New York: Teachers College Press.

Office for Standards in Education (OFSTED). 1993. *Boys and English*. London: Her Majesty's Stationery Office.

———. 1998. *Secondary Education 1993–1997: A Review of Secondary Schools in England*. London: The Stationery Office.

Penny, Val. 1998. "Raising Boys' Achievement in English: How an Action Research Approach Had a Major Impact on Boys' Literacy at the Wakeman School in Shrewsbury." In *Raising Boys' Achievement in Schools*, ed. Kevan Bleach. Stoke on Trent: Trentham.

Pike, Mark. 2000. "Pupils' Poetics." *Changing English* 7.1: 45–54.

Pipher, Mary. 1994. *Reviving Ophelia: Saving the Selves of Adolescent Girls*. New York: Ballantine.

Pirie, Bruce. 1997. *Reshaping High School English*. Urbana, IL: National Council of Teachers of English.

Pollack, William. 1998. *Real Boys: Rescuing Our Sons from the Myths of Boyhood*. New York: Random House.

Pope, Harrison G. Jr., Katharine A. Phillips, and Roberto Olivardia. 2000. *The Adonis Complex: The Secret Crisis of Male Body Obsession*. New York: Free.

Pottorff, Donald D., Deborah Phelps-Zientarski, and Michele E. Skovera. 1996. "Gender Perceptions of Elementary and Middle School Students About Literacy at School and Home." *Journal of Research and Development in Education* 29.4: 203–11.

Pugh, Kate. 1995. "Boys and English: Classroom Voices." *The English & Media Magazine* 33: 19–20.

Qualifications and Curriculum Authority (QCA). 1998. *Can Do Better: Raising Boys' Achievement in English*. London: QCA.

Rosenblatt, Louise M. 1978. *The Reader the Text the Poem: The Transactional Theory of the Literary Work*. Carbondale and Edwardsville, IL: Southern Illinois University Press.

Sadker, Myra, and David Sadker. 1994. *Failing at Fairness: How America's Schools Cheat Girls*. New York: Scribners.

Salisbury, Jonathan, and David Jackson. 1996. *Challenging Macho Values: Practical Ways of Working with Adolescent Boys*. London: Falmer.

Schaal, Benoist, Richard E. Tremblay, Robert Soussignan, and Elizabeth J. Susman. 1996. "Male Testosterone Linked to High Social Dominance but Low Physical Aggression in Early Adolescence." *Journal of the American Academy of Child and Adolescent Psychiatry* 35.10: 1322–30.

Skelton, Christine. 2001. *Schooling the Boys: Masculinities and Primary Education*. Buckingham: Open University Press.

Sommers, Christina Hoff. 2000. *The War Against Boys: How Misguided Feminism Is Harming Our Young Men*. New York: Simon & Shuster.

Spin City. 2000. DreamWorks. ABC-TV. 24 May.

Stigler, James W., and James Hiebert. 1999. *The Teaching Gap: Best Ideas from the World's Teachers for Improving Education in the Classroom*. New York: Free.

Styslinger, Mary E. 1999. "Mars and Venus in My Classroom: Men Go to Their Caves and Women Talk During Peer Revision." *English Journal* 88.3: 50–56.

Sumara, Dennis. 2000. "Learning to Say Something True About the World." In *Advocating Change: Contemporary Issues in Subject English*, ed. Barrie R. C. Barrell and Roberta F. Hammett. Toronto: Irwin.

Tannen, Deborah. 1990. *You Just Don't Understand: Women and Men in Conversation*. New York: Ballantine.

Teese, Richard, Merryn Davies, Margaret Charlton, and John Polesel. 1995. *Who Wins at School? Boys and Girls in Australian Secondary Education*. Melbourne: Department of Education Policy and Management, University of Melbourne.

Thomas, Peter. 1997. "Doom to the Red-Eyed Nyungghns from the Planet Glarg: Boys as Writers of Narrative." *English in Education* 31.3: 23–31.

Thorne, Barrie. 1993. *Gender Play: Girls and Boys in School*. New Brunswick, NJ: Rutgers University Press.

Tough Guise: Violence, Media, and the Crisis in Masculinity, with Jackson Katz. 1999. Abridged version. Dir. Sut Jhally. Northampton, MA: Media Education Foundation.

Vygotsky, Lev S. 1978. *Mind in Society: The Development of Higher Psychological Processes*, ed. Michael Cole, Vera John-Steiner, Sylvia Scribner, and Ellen Souberman. Cambridge MA: Harvard University Press.

Watching TV. 1994. Dir. Christopher Hinton. National Film Board of Canada. Included on *Scanning Television: Videos for Media Literacy in Class*. 1997. Face to Face Media. Toronto: Harcourt Brace.

Watt, Helen M. G., and Jacquelynne S. Eccles. 1999. "An International Comparison of Students' Maths- and English-Related Perceptions Through High School Using Hierarchical Linear Modeling." Paper presented at the joint conference of the Australian Association for

Research in Education and the New Zealand Association for Research in Education, 29 November–2 December, Melbourne, Australia.

Wilhelm, Jeffrey D. 1997. *"You Gotta BE the Book": Teaching Engaged and Reflective Reading with Adolescents*. New York: Teachers College Press, and Urbana, IL: National Council of Teachers of English.

Wilhelm, Jeffrey D., Tanya N. Baker, and Julie Dube. 2001. *Strategic Reading: Guiding Students to Lifelong Literacy, 6–12*. Portsmouth, NH: Boynton/Cook.

Williams, Raymond. 1977. *Marxism and Literature*. Oxford: Oxford University Press.